FESTIVALS AND FEAST DAYS OF LINCOLNSHIRE

BY

MABEL PEACOCK

SECTION I.

FESTIVALS.

New Year.—If the first person who enters a house on New-year's morning bring bad news, it is a sign of ill-luck for the whole of the year. As soon as the clock strikes twelve on New-year's morning bring something indoors, for it is lucky to have some incoming before there is any outgoing.—E. PEACOCK, i., 179.

Bring a bit of green into the house on New-year's day, and you won't want bread all the year ; or, if you do, some one will bring you some. You must not bring in anything dead, or you bring a coffin into the house. Whatever you bring in first on New Year's Day, you will never want all the year through, so the custom is to bring in coals or something useful.—COLE, p. 98.

The New Year will be marked by death or ill-luck if fire be taken out of the house, or if nothing green be taken in, or if the first-foot be a woman or a fair man instead of a dark man.—*Bygone Lincolnshire*, ii., 94.

The 'first-foot' belief of the Scotch on New Year's Day does not come down so far as Lincolnshire, but we knew an old farmer and his niece who always took care on that day to be the first to leave the house, and to return with something in their hands—an egg, a flower, or piece of holly.—*Antiquary*, xiv., 12.

Festivals.

Bottesford. Mr. Watkins is in error when he says that 'the "first-foot" belief of the Scotch on New Year's Day does not come down so far as Lincolnshire.' An old friend of mine tells me that she would not on any account let a woman or girl enter her house before a man or boy had crossed the threshold on that day. 'I alus keäp dōōr lock'd till reight soort cums, an' then I saay, "Hev' yĕ owt to bring in? If yĕ hevn't goa get a bit o' stick or sum'ats, ye sea it's straange an' unlucky to tak things oot afore owt's browt in, an' foaks is careful. I mind th' time when lads cum'd roond reg'lar wi' bits o' stick aboot as long as a knittin' needle." '—*Antiquary*, xiv., 86.

Lincolnshire Marsh. There is still many a house in Marshland where much is thought of the first-foot which crosses the threshold on the New Year's morning; that first-foot must be a light-haired, fair-complexioned man. First-foot must bring something in with him, and on no account may anything be taken out of the house till something has been brought in :

> Take out, then take in ; bad luck will begin.
> Take in, then take out, good luck comes about.

HEANLEY, p. 7.

Mumby. 'We reckon to have a log on New Year's Eve,' remarked a parishioner, and my aunt at Lincoln, when I was staying there, said, 'You must see first of all on a New Year's morning, one of the opposite sex (not a member of your own family).' Boys go round and wish the women a Happy New Year, adding 'and I've brought you a bit of stick.' Girls do the same to the men, and both expect rewards, in the shape of current coin. Many people are most particular to open a Bible first of all, saying that the verse the eye first rests on (or thumb touches) foretells what the new year will be. A piece of green is also to be brought in and placed in the Bible. It is very unlucky to see the new moon for the first time through glass. Whatever you do on New

Year's Day you ll be doing all the year.—L. N. & Q., vol. ii., p. 139.

New Year Ringings.—NORTH, pp. 226-232.

Kyme. It is a trait of character which had not expired in the middle of the last century, that the lower classes pertinaciously retained the custom of converting most of the old festivals into a holiday. Thus William Hall, the Kyme water poet, who was born about that period says— ' I perfectly remember, old Mr. Anthony Peacock, uncle to the late Anthony Peacock, Esq. threatening to horse-whip Frank Pears, the tailor, because he would not go to mend the great mill (Engiven) sail-cloths on old Christmas day.' In the present age it is scarcely known by the same class of people when old Christmas day arrives.—OLIVER (3), p. 4, footnote.

Grantham. There was generally gaiety astir on Twelfth Night, the parting hour of Christmastide. We youngsters were once (perhaps twice) asked to a party where some of the amusement provided consisted in ' drawing for characters.' A bag filled with folded papers was handed round and each of us was invited to take one, which on being opened was found to be a roughly coloured print of Sir Tilbury Nogo, Miss Fanny Fanciful, or some such personage whose character we might assume, and to whose name we were called upon to answer for the rest of the evening, during which we ought to have paid especial respect to the boy or girl whose luck had made them King and Queen. I do not believe this was at all a Grantham custom at the time [in the Fifties] of which I speak, though it may have been so when our hostess (who had grand-children about her) was in her prime. G. J., June 29, 1878.

Epiphany.—See HAXEY HOOD-GAME, PART II., SECTION III., GAMES.

Addlethorpe.
I. Itm. reseuyd apo ploughe day -   -   iij*s.* iij*d.*
Addlethorpe Churchwarden's Accounts, A.D. 1542.—
OLDFIELD, p. 110.

Holbeach.
       It. to Wm. Davy the sygne whereon the plowghe
          did stond -   -   -   -   -   -   xvj.
A Boake of the Stuffe in the Cheyrche of Holbeach
[1547].—*Church Furniture,* p. 237.

Leverton. *Plough Light.—*
     1498.   Resseuyd of ye plowth lyth of leuton   xl*s.*
                                  LEVERTON, p. 6.

     1526.   Of Thomas Sledman of benyngton for debt of
Robert warner to ye plough lyght   -   -   -   xx*d.*
                               LEVERTON, p. 17.

     1531 [?].   Of Thomas burton for debt of ye plow-
       lyght   -   -   -   -   -   -   xx*d.*
                               LEVERTON, p. 21.

     1557.   ℞ of John Bushe and adlard Greyne for the
       sopper light   -   -   -   -   -   x*s.*
     1558.   ℞ vpon plugh muday for sopperes light ij*s* v*d.*
     1559.   Resaued of willyam Wastlare jun & John
       pullw'tofte of the plowygh lyght mone   -   xvij*d.*
                         LEVERTON, pp. 29-30.
Plough Monday [?]—
     1577.   Rec^d of the Plowe maysters   -   xxij*s* viij*d.*
                             LEVERTON, p. 33.

     1611.   For ayle on plowmunday   -   -   xij*d*
                             LEVERTON, p. 36.
Louth.
       Item. for xxiiij*li* wax to Robert Bayly for iiij tapers
          to bere abowt the sacrament bowght with mony
          gatherd on plowghe monday and syns   -   xij*s.*
Excerpts from the Parish Books.—*Notitiæ Ludæ,* p. 48.

Festivals.

Plough-Light.—Frequent are the allusions in the Parish Registers to the plowlight, a word which, after much inquiry, I think may mean a tribute gathered by, or for the plowmen, and is synonymous with plowalms, as the following sentence intimates :—'de qualibet caruca juncta inter Pascha et Pentecostem unum denarium qui dicitur Plowalmes,' *apud Sanctum Ivonem.* Or the word plowlight may signify a taper kept at the expense, and in behalf of the plowmen near the holy sepulchre, a custom by no means uncommon. . . .

I have nothing to add, further than quoting some of the passages where the word plowlight occurs in the Register :

'Memd. that there was gather'd of the plowelighte
mony   -   -   -   -   -   viijs. x*d*.
Whereof paid to the ploughe men -   -   -   ijs.
Item. Payde to Thomas Wollarby for the plowe
lyght   -   -   -   -   -   -   iijs.
'Also paid to the ploo lyght   -   -   -   xvj*d*.
Mem. That William Glew hathe gyven this yeare a reede to the lightyng of the sepulchre light, and other lyghts in the chirche, conteynyng v yardes of the lengthe.'

After the destruction of the altars, guilds, processions, and many of the festivals of the papal church, there was no station or trimmer for the plowlight, and the custom died of . . . neglect.—*Notitiæ Ludæ*, pp. 220, 221.

Sutterton. 1490. Among the receipts this year occurs a sum of x*s* paid by 'Thomas Raffyn of ye plowlyth.' This plough-light was no doubt the lamp of one of the parish gilds. There was a plough-light at Leverton, near Boston, and another at Louth. There was a plough gild at Kirton in Lindsey and in many other places. The following entry was to be seen in the church accounts of Holbeach ; it occurs in a list of church goods disposed of by the wardens in 1549 : 'To Wm. Davy, the sygne whereon the plowyghe did stand.'* It would seem from this that a plough was one of the ornaments with which that church was decorated. Probably it hung on the wall in some conspicuous place near to the gild-altar. —E. PEACOCK, *Churchwardens' Accounts of Saint Mary's, Sutterton*, p. 3.

The receipts for this year [1525] shew that there were five lights in the church exclusive of that before the high altar. They were called the May-light, the ' Hognar's '-light, the Plough-light, the Sepulchre-light, and All Soul's-light.—*Ib.* p. 10.

Waddington. In the old Churchwarden's Book of Waddington there is under the date 1642, the appointment of four persons as ' Plowmeisters.' These appointments continue to be entered annually for about a hundred years. It further appears that these plough masters had in their hands certain monies called plough money, which they undertook to produce on plough-day (*i.e.* first Monday after Twelfth Day). The form of undertaking is as follows :

' Andrew Newcome hath in his hands the sum of xx^s and hath promised to bringe the Stocke upon plow-daye next, and hath hereto sett his hande ' (1642).

And ninety-six years later :

' Memorandum that John Foxe hath in his hands £2 10 of the Plow-money which sum I acknowledge myself indebted to the town of Waddington ' (1738).

Occasionally there are undertakings to bring in the rent or interest of it as well as the ' stock ' or principal, and it would seem that some of it at least was spent in a festal manner, as on Jan. 7th, 1706, there is an entry :

' On plow-day ye 7 January paid to the Ringers and						
Minstrels	-	-	-	-	-	1	4
Spent at the same time		-	-	-	1	9

* Marrat, ' *Hist. Linc.*,' ii., 104.

Festivals.

I should be thankful if some one more learned than myself in Ecclesiology would explain when and where the 'Ploweth' light was usually lit. Was it at Rogation-tide, when the coming crops were prayed for, or was it on what we still call Plough Monday?—L. N. & Q., vol. iii., p. 47.

Wainfleet. Item to the Ploweth lyght there vid. [The *there* referring to the church of our Lady, Wainfleet.] *The Will of Robert Barret, of Wainfleet made April 28th,* 1527.—L. N. & Q., vol. iii., p. 48.

Wigtoft [1532].
fyrst recevid of *John atkynson* and *Robt Shepperd,* for the plowght lyght - - - - 1 6 8
Accompts of Churchwardens, p. 219.
Wigtoft [1535].
Itm. recevyd of yᵉ plowght lyght - - 1 6 8
Accompts of Churchwardens, p. 226.

Wigtoft. *Plough-gathering* [1575].—
Receid of *Wyllm clarke* & *John Waytt,* of yᵉ plougadrin - - - - - - 1 0 0
Accompts of Churchwardens, p. 240.

Bully-buck.—A fool in the game of Plough-bullocks.— E. PEACOCK, II., vol. i., p. 47.

Besom Bet—A plough-boy who at 'plough-jagging' time impersonates an old woman with a besom.—E. PEACOCK, i., p. 22.

Blether-Dick.—A character among mummers.—E. PEACOCK, II., vol. i., p. 56.

Plough-jags.—Hobby-herse.—One of the 'plough-jags' dressed so as to look like a horse.—E. PEACOCK, II., vol. i., p. 273.

I. of Axholme. *Largus, i.e. largesse.*—The cry of the plough-jags, when they go from house to house to perform and beg.—Cf. PECK, *Acc. of Isle of Axholme,* 278 ; E. PEACOCK, i., p. 153.

Festivals.

One of the mummers in the Lincolnshire Plough Monday Procession usually wears a fox's skin, in the form of a hood, and 'Bessy' a bullock's tail under her gown, which he holds in his hand when dancing.—P. H. DITCHFIELD, *Old English Customs*, 1896, p. 49.

Axholme. The plough-jacks on Plough Monday come round dressed like morris-dancers with the fool as 'Billy Buck,' a boy as the maiden, two rival suitors, and another as the old witch in a red cloak with a besom, with which she sweeps them all out, after the play is ended. Sometimes they come with horse-cloths over their heads and ride 'hobby-horse,' and this often leads to horse-play, and fights used to take place between the rival parties of villages on the opposite sides of the Trent.—ANDERSON, p. 79.

Plough-boys.—Country-men, who go about dressed in ribbon, etc., as 'Morris (Moorish) dancers on Plough Monday, perform the sword-dance, etc. One is dressed as 'Maid Marion,' and is called the witch, another in rags, and is called the fool, etc., etc.—THOMPSON, p. 718.

Plough-boys,   Plough-bullocks,   Plough-jags.—Morris Dancers.

Plough Bullocks are characters now almost unknown, but there are persons living who well remember these itinerant Thespians, about the period of Plough Monday (Jan. 8th), exhibiting their performance wherever they found people's doors not barred against them. Like the mummers of the 'olden tyme,' they had the wild man and the jester combined in one character, who, with his conical cap, and in a dress entirely covered with shreds of various coloured cloth, seemed to be the chief *persona dramatis.* Another character designated 'Sweet Sis,' was undertaken by one of the more juvenile of the company, and a third named 'old Joan,' both habited in female costume, the former to represent an attractive young lady, and the latter a repulsive, brazen-faced woman, were the most conspicuous performers. The others, some half-dozen youths, having their rustic attire covered with bunches of gaudy-coloured ribbons, being merely supernumeraries. The blundering manner in which each performed his part, made the plot or theme almost unintelligible, except that the former of the two lady characters, by her fastidiousness, lost her lover (he in shreds with a conical cap) whom the coarse homeliness of 'old Joan' won. The amount collected by these plough-bullocks was often considerable, and was expended in giving a treat to their friends, male and female. These rustic balls gave rise to results that caused their suppression, and the custom of maurice dancing or plough-jagging (another name it had) ceased. —BROGDEN, pp. 151, 152.

Plough-jags.—The following dialogue [is] used by plough-jags in some parts of the country.

The principal characters are Beelzebub, a fool, a doctor, a woman and baby, a soldier, a collector, etc.

They commence by singing outside a house :

'Good master and good mistress,
    As you sit by the fire,
Remember us poor plough-boys
    Who travel through muck and mire.
The mire is so deep : we travel far and near
To wish you a happy and prosperous New Year.'

The fool knocks and asks permission to show their play as follows :

'In comes I, Tom Fool,
    The biggest fool you've ever seen ;
There's five more little boys out here,
    By your consent they shall come in.'

Leave having been obtained he bids them 'step up.' The soldier enters first and sings a song which appears

to be *ad lib.* ; I can hear of no particular words. Next
enters one of the company dressed as a woman.

> *Woman.* In comes I, old Dame Jane,
> With a neck as long as a crane,
> Long have I sought thee, now I've found thee :
> Tommy, bring the baby in.
> > *[Lad hands her a sham baby.*
> > *Enter* BEELZEBUB.

> *Beelzebub.* In comes I, old Beelzebub,
> In my hand I carry my club,
> Under my arm a whit-leather dripping pan,
> Don't you think me a funny old man?

Is there any old woman in this company who dare stand before
me?

> *Woman.* Yes, me.   *[Beelzebub knocks her down.*
> *Fool.* Beelzebub, Beelzebub, what hast thou done !
> Killed poor old dame Jane and lamed her son.
> Five pounds for a doctor !
> *Beelzebub.* Ten to stop away.
> *Fool.* Fifteen to come in in a case like this.
> > *Enter* DOCTOR.
> *Doctor.* In comes I, the Doctor.
> *Fool.* How became you a doctor?
> *Doctor.* I travelled for it.
> *Fool.* Where did you travel?
> *Doctor.* England, France, Ireland, Spain,
> Now I've come to doctor England again.
> *Fool.* What diseases can you cure?
> *Doctor.* Hipsy, pipsy, palsy, and gout,
> Pains within and pains without,
> Heal the sick, and cure the lame,
> Raise the dead to life again.
> *Fool.* Now try your skill.
> > *[Doctor takes hold of Woman's ankle.*
> *Fool.* Is that where her pulse lies?
> *Doctor.* Yes, the finest and most delicate part about a lady. Her

pulse beats nineteen times to the tick of my watch once.

> This woman is not dead, but in a trance,
> If she can't dance we can't sing,
> So raise her up and let's begin.
> > *[The Collector here takes the hat round
> > while the others dance about.*

M

The fool leaves first, when the others sing as follows:

> Good master and good mistress,
> You see our fool is gone,
> We make it up in business
> To follow him along.
> We thank you for civility
> And all you gave us here,
> We wish you all, good night,
> And a prosperous new year.
>
> *[Exeunt omnes.*

The soldier is always introduced decked with streaming ribbons.—L. N. & Q., vol. ii., pp. 88, 89.

Hibaldstow. The hundred years which have just concluded witnessed the disappearance of several ancient customs, but the Plough Monday pageant has survived into the twentieth century, though not without modification. The North Lincolnshire 'plough-jags,' for instance, have gone from house to house this season fantastically attired; and if they no longer drag the plough of olden times with them, they are still sometimes accompanied by a fiery and curveting hobby-horse. It may perhaps be worth while to enshrine the following version of the 'ditties' recited by the mummers in the pages of 'N. & Q.,' for who knows how long or how short a time may elapse before they are discarded and forgotten?

The following dialogue is printed as written down for Miss Fowler of Winterton, by W. A., from the dictation of his father, who lives in the parish of Hibaldstow. It contains one interesting idiom, 'War out!' which Miss Fowler herself takes down in another version as 'Where out!' The words appear to mean 'Be wary!' 'Pay attention!' 'Look out!' or, as Lincolnshire people frequently exclaim, 'Mind yersens!' Otherwise the only noteworthy thing about the rime is that the combat which should occur is omitted, and consequently no doctor appears to bring the fallen champion to life.

Festivals.

PLOUGHBOYS.

Clown, (1st actor).

Good evening, ladys and Gentlemen,
  I am making rather a bole call;
But Christmas time is a merry time,
  I have come to see you all.
I hope you will not be ofended
  For what I have got to say:
Here is a few more jolly fellows
  Will step in this way.

Soldier, No. 2nd.

I am a Recruited seagent
  Arriving here just now:
My orders is to enlist all
  Who follow the cart and plough.

Foreign Traveller, 3rd.

O endeed, mr seagant,
  As I suppose you are,
You want us bold malishal lads
  To face the Boer war.
Will (We'll) boldly face the enemy
  And do the best we can,
And if they dont prove civil
  We will slay them every one.
I am a Foreign traveller,
  I have travelled land and sea,
And nothing do I want but a wife
To please me the rest part of my life.

Lady, 4th.

I am a lady bright and gay,
  The fortune of my charm,
And scornfully I'm thrown away
  Into my lover arms.

3rd (i.e. the Foreign Traveller).

I have meet my dearest jewel;
  She is the comforts of my life,
And if she proves true to me
  I entend her been my wife.

Festivals.

Farmer, 5th.

Madam, it is my desire,
 If I should be the man
All for to gain your fancy, love,
 I will do the best I can.
I have got both corn and cattle,
 And everything you know,
Besides a team of horses
 To draw along the plough.

Lady.

Young man you are deceitful,
 As any of the rest ;
So for for (*sic*) that reason I will have
 Them I love best.

Soilder (sic).

Come me lads, who is bound for listing,
 And gan along with me ;
You shall have all kinds of liquor
 While you are in our company.

Indian King, No. 6.

War out ! me lads, and let me come in !
For I am the old chap called Indian King.
They all have been trying me to slay ;
But you see I am alive to this very day.

Hoby Horse, No. 7.

In comes a four year old cout,
 A fine as ever was bought :
He can hotch and he can trot
 14 miles in 15 hours just like nought.

Lady Jane No. 8.

In comes Jane with a long leg crayn
Rambling over the midow :
Once I was a blouming young girl,
 But now I am a down old widow.

No 2 (*i.e. the Soldier*).

Gentlemen, and ladies,
 You seen our fool is gone ;
We'll make it our business
 To follow him along ;

Festivals.

> We thank you for civility
>   That you have shown us here;
> We wish you a merry Christmas
>   And a happy new year.

The introductory speech of the clown given below differs from that in the above dialogue. It was copied by Miss Mina Fowler from the version of a village boy in Winterton, but the rest of the 'ditties' have still to be collected.

> In comes I, ohs (I've?) never been before,
> With my big head and my little wit.
> If my head be big and my wit be small
> I'll act Tomfool among you all.
> Ah, Ah, Ah, you and me,
> Little brown juden (jug?), I love thee,
> If I had a cow that gave such milk
> I'll clothe her in the richest silk.
> I'll feed her on the best of hay,
> And milk her forty times a day.
> In comes I, hungry and dry,
> Please will you give us a bit of pork-pie.

The request which concludes this speech smacks of the soil, for pork-pie is a favourite dish among high and low in the county of Tennyson and Newton, where 'pig-meat' is held in great esteem.

N. Lincolnshire Wolds. The next dialogue was repeated to Miss Fowler at Winterton by Mrs. I., who gave it as used on 'the hillside' (the western slope of the wolds in North Lincolnshire) some twenty-five years ago. It is to be noticed that in this version, as in the one from Hibaldstow, the hobby-horse can 'hotch,' whatever pace that word may mean, while a long-legged crane is again referred to in 'Jane's' speech. It may be that the heron, not the true crane, has suggested the line. The latter bird is now only a chance visitor, while the former is, or was till lately, sometimes called the crane, its more common name being heronsew. The 'Doctor's' part includes an allusion to bagpipes (here possibly a comic name for the lungs), which were once well-known instruments of music in the county. An old man who could play the Lincolnshire pipes was still living in the neighbourhood of Kirton-in-Lindsey in the earlier half of the nineteenth century, but both the player and his pipes have now vanished.

PLOUGH-JAGS' DITTIES.

The Hobby-Horse.

Here comes a four-year-old colt (cowt)
As fine a filly as ever was bought (bowt)
He can 'otch an' he can trot,
An' he can carry a butter-pot
Nine miles high wi'out touching the sky.

Jane, or Besom Betty.

In comes Jane with a long-legged crane,
 Creeping over the meadow ;
Once I was a blooming maid,
 But now a down owd widow.
                    (She sweeps about with her broom.)

The Soldier.

I'm a recruiting serjeant
 Arrived 'ere just now ;
My orders are to 'list all
 That follow cart and plough,
Likewise fiddlers, tinkers,
 And all that can advance.
 I should like to see our fool dance.
Ah ! but I can sing.
Come all you lads, that's a mind for listin'
Come with me and be not afraid :
You shall have all kinds of liquor,
 Likewise dance with a pretty maid.

The Fool

is supposed to kill one of the men, and then they shout, 'Dead ! and where's the doctor?'

The Doctor.

Here I am, the doctor ;
 I can cure the itch, the stitch
 The blind, the lame,
 And raise the dead to life again.

I once cured a man that had been in his grave nine years.
Take hold of my bottle till I feel his pulse—
And every time he stirr'd his bagpipes played—
Cheer up, Sam, and let's have a dance.

The Indian King.

(He appears as a black man with a white dress.)
Where out! my lads, let me come in,
I'm the chap they call 'the Indian King.'

The Lady.

I'm a lady bright and gay,
The truth to you I'll tell.

. . . . .

What did the Fool say?

. . . . .

Kirton-in-Lindsey. The following variant of the play, which was written down for me by J. H., a Kirton-in-Lindsey man, who before his marriage used to be one of the performers, contains the word 'sleve' in connexion with a hat :

And not much *sleve* left in the lining.

'Sleave-silk' or 'sleave' formerly meant the soft floss-silk used for weaving. . . . In the plough-jag's play it would seem to signify either silken fabric, or the nap on such a fabric when woven with a satin-like surface.

PART I.

Good evening, ladies and gentlemen all,
Xmas being a merry time
We thought we would give you a call :
And if you will listen
To what I've got to say,
For in a short time there will be
Some more pretty boys and girls this way.
Some can dance and some can sing ;
By your consent they shall come in.

PART II.

In comes a recruiting seargant,
As I suppose you are.
You want some bold malitia men,
To face the rageing war.

Festivals.

We will bravely face the enemy,
And do the best we can,
And if they don't prove civil,
We will slay them every man.

PART III. (*Lady sings.*)
In comes a lady bright and gay,
Good fortunes and sweet charms ;
I've scornfully being thrown away
Out of some lover's arms.
He swears if I don't wed with him,
As you all understand,
He'll list all for a soldier,
And go to some foreign land.

First Man says,

Pray madam if them be his thoughts
.   .   .   .   . let him go,
He never meanes to wed with you,
But prove your overthrow.
When poverty once begins to pinch,
In which it will some day,
He'll have another sweetheart
And with her he'll run away.

Lady.

Thank you, kind sir, for your advice
Which you have given to me.
I never meant to wed with him,
But have him for to know
I'll have another sweetheart
And along with him I'll go.

4th Man.

In comes I, King George,
With courage stout and bold :
With this bright sword I won
Ten thousand pounds in gold.
I fought a fiery dragon,
And brought him to the slaughter,
And by that means I won
The queen's eldest daughter.
I 'ashed him and smashed him as small as flies,
And sent him to jamacia to make mince-pies.

.

Festivals.

2nd Man says,

Thou 'ashed me and smashed me as small as flies,
And sent me to jamacia to make mince-pies.
Hold thy lies or my blood will rise !
If thou art the King I dare face the.

Then arises a duel between the 2nd man and the King. The
King knocks the 2nd man down.

King.

Five pounds for a Dr.

Dr.

No Dr. under ten.

King.

Ten pounds for a Dr.

Dr.

In comes I, the Dr.

King.

How comes you to be the Dr.?

Dr.

By my travels.

King.

Where have you travelled from?

Dr.

From the fireside to the bedside, and from the bedside to the
old corner cupboard, where there I have had many a nice bit of
pork-pie and mince-pie, that makes me such a bold fellow as I am.

King.

What can you cure?

Dr.

Almost anything.

The itch, the pitch, the palsy, gout,
Pains within, and aches without.

If this man 'as got 19 diseases within him I will fetch 21 out.
Take hold of this bottle while I feel on this mans pulse.

King.

Where do you feel on his pulse?

Dr.

Where it beats the strongest.

This man's not dead he his only in a trance
Rise up my good man and have a dance.

(The lady and the 2nd man dances.)

Festivals.

6th Man.

In comes poor old lame Jane
  Leaping over the meadow ;
Once I was a blooming girl,
  But now I am a down old widow.
You see my old hat his boath greacey and fat,
  And that you can tell by the shineing ;
There his holes in the crown, and holes all round,
  And not much sleve left in the lineing.

Then all sing.

Good master, and good mistress,
  As you sit round the fire,
Remember us poor plough-boys
  That go through mud and mire :
The mire is so deep,
  And the water runs so clear :
We wish you a merry Xmas,
  And a happy New Year.

When a portion of this play was acted by very young
lads a few years ago, 'the Doctor,' who then found the
patient's pulse in his shin, wore a top hat that was much
too large. This imposing headgear lent him an appearance which was all that could be desired when it was held
up by his ears, but at certain disastrous moments these
supports would fail, and sudden eclipse overtake the
actor. It must be owned, however, that while wrestling
with the difficulties thus caused, and throughout the whole
scene, he like his companions succeeded in preserving a
funereal gravity of deportment. It was only from the
sense of the words uttered, not from intonation or gesture,
the spectators could gather that they were witnessing a
drama which had been conceived in a certain spirit of
levity. Even the allusion to pork-pie failed to evoke a
gleam of animation.

The wife of J. H., who supplied this dialogue, was once
much alarmed when she was a girl living as servant at
Walton-le-Dale, near Tattershall, for a man disguised as

a sheep (see Christmas Tup, 9th S., ii., 511) opened the outer door of the house, in which she happened to be alone. He was one of a set of plough-jags; but she could not describe his mates and their costumes, for, startled and afraid she 'banged the door to,' to keep the gang from entering. Usually 'the lady,' 'lame Jane,' who represents a rough old woman with a besom, 'the soldier,' and 'the king' are dressed with some regard to character. The plough-jags with no spoken parts, who used to be the bullocks drawing the plough, or sometimes sword players, it may be, should, properly speaking, wear very tall beribboned hats, with white shirts over their other clothes. These shirts should also be trimmed with ribbons and other ornaments; but the garments are seldom seen now—perhaps because white linen shirts are at present rarely kept for wearing on high days and holidays by the men themselves, or by the friends from whom they can borrow. The fool should be dressed in skins, or in snippets of brightly coloured rags, and should be armed with a bladder at the end of a whip, or some such weapon.—N. & Q.⁹, vol. vii., pp. 322, 323, 324, 363, 364.

St. Agnes'-Eve [Jan. 20].—See SECTION VII.

Candlemas Day [Feb. 2].—Any goose falls to lay by Old Candlemas Day—in allusion to the saying :—

New Candlemas Day, good goose will lay:
Old Candlemas Day, any goose will lay.

COLE, p. 44.

Valentine's Day.—On the 14th of February we duly sent and received 'vollantines'—*val*entines we set down as an alien affectation. One verse which we were fond of scrawling to each other is too universally known for me to venture to quote: it refers to the redness of the rose, the blueness of the violet [etc.]. . . . But there was another favourite which I will not withhold, as it refers to the significance of colours, a subject of no small interest :

> " If you love me, love me true ;
> Send me a ribbon, and let it be blue.
> If you hate me let it be seen ;
> Send me a ribbon, and let it be green."

G.. J., June 29, 1878.

Valentine's Day is dead and gone. The modern Christmas cards have all but supplied the place of the missives, some of them very coarse and vulgar, which were common enough twenty years ago, *i.e.* 1879, and I do not think that at any time Valentine's Day had in Marshland the importance it had further north.—HEANLEY, p. 7.

Brusting Saturday.—The Saturday before Shrove Tuesday, on which day frying-pan pudding is eaten.

This is made of the same material as pancake, but is thicker, and of a crumbling character.—BROGDEN, p. 31.

Pharson's Tuesday is given as a synonym for Shrove Tuesday in an article, ' From the Heart of the Wolds' (Lincolnshire), in the *Cornhill Magazine* for August, 1882.—N. & Q.⁶, vol. vi., p. 166.

[' Pharson's ' said to be a mistake for *Fastens.— Ib.* p. 334.]

Pan-cake Bell.—C. NORTH, pp. 214-219, 282, 519, 658.

Fritters.—Puffs or pancakes made with apples (cut up) or fruit in them. *Ex.* We'll have fritters on Shrove Tuesday.—BROGDEN, p. 74.

Flap-jack.—A very large pan-cake. *Ex.* I'll have a flap-jack on Fasten Tuesday.—BROGDEN, p. 70.

In Lincolnshire the first pancake which the farmer's wife fries on Shrove Tuesday is given to the cock in the crewyard. Old wives cannot be persuaded to fry another cake until one has been given to the cock. The daughter of the house watches the ceremony, and as many hens as come to help the cock to eat the pancake so many years she will remain unwed.—ADDY, p. 65.

Grantham. Shrove Tuesday was the orthodox day for beginning top-whipping and battledore and shuttlecock-playing ; these toys might be practised upon a week or so in advance, but that, I presume, was only like hunting in October, and did not count. To most of us pancakes were the *raison d'être* of the day, and we eagerly listened for a bell which sounded from the church steeple some-time during the morning, and was, we were told, a signal specially designed to warn house-wives to prepare their batter. This so-called 'pancake-bell' was, if I do not mistake, independent of the daily call to Matins.—G. J., June 29, 1878.

[See PART II., SECTION III., for GAMES PLAYED ON SHROVE-TUESDAY, including COCK-FIGHTING.]

Shrove-Tuesday.—See PART II., SECTION I. for 'SAINT RATTLE DOLL FAIR, CROWLAND.

Ash Wednesday was a festival in our esteem, for we feasted on apple-fritters.—G. J., June 29, 1878.

Huttoft neighbourhood. '*Clerk Thursday.*'—The name is given to the day following 'Ash Wednesday,' and the school children consider themselves entitled to trick (or even force) the teacher into leaving the schoolroom, when they bolt the door and refuse admittance until a holiday has been granted for the rest of the day.—L. N. & Q., vol. iii., p. 122.

Grantham.—Allen's *History of the County of Lincoln*, vol. ii., p. 308, states that the fair held at Grantham on the Monday before Palm Sunday for horses, horned cattle and sheep is called 'caring fair.' The appellation is derived from the old name by which the Sunday before Palm Sunday was popularly known, viz., Care Sunday.— N. & Q.[8], vol. iv., p. 168.

Festivals.

Crowland. Knives given away on St. Bartholomew's day.—*Hist. and Antiq. of Croyland Abbey*, pp. 73, 77.

Palm-Sunday.—Palms, the flowers of a kind of willow, so called because they were formerly used instead of palms on Palm-Sunday.—E. PEACOCK, i., p. 187.

Pussy-Paums.—The Catkins of the Sallow; the so-called Palm or Paum; sometimes called Goslings.—COLE, p. 114.

Lent.—In Lincolnshire it is supposed that the catkins ought always to be in bloom by the fifth Sunday in Lent, and children search for them in places where the willow grows; but when Easter falls early, and the season has been a cold and backward one, they are often almost impossible to find in the eastern and northern counties. —*Dublin Review*, 1898, p. 145.

Lincolnshire Marshland. *Good Friday.*—It is worth while noting that, whereas throughout most northern counties it is still deemed most impious to disturb the earth in any way then, and seeds sown on that day will never thrive; yet, in Marshland, Good Friday is the day of all days in the year on which to plant potatoes and sow peas, inasmuch as on that day the soil was redeemed from the power of the Evil one.* But, on the other hand, I have a distinct recollection of a Good Friday afternoon when one of our horses had cast a shoe in driving to Skegness Church, and the blacksmith there flatly refused to put another on, for 'owd Scrat 'ud hev' him sartain sewer, if 'e put hand to hammer or nails the whole blessed daa'—a distinct influence from the terrible purpose to which they had been put on the first Good Friday.—HEANLEY, p. 8.

* In North West Lincolnshire, too, potatoes are often set on Good Friday, and other gardening is readily done. I never heard a theological reason given for the practice, however.

Festivals.

At Kirton-in-Lindsey it [the cross] seems to be formed by merely drawing a knife twice across the top of the bun ; in some places stamps are used, and in my childhood at Bottesford, I can remember seeing them made by pricking out a cross with a three pronged fork, thus :

Dublin Review, 1898, p. 148.

Good Friday we usually called Hot Cross Bun Day. . . . I used to wonder how the buns got their name, for I never saw a cross upon them : their shape was always triangular, and that, I believe, was their only peculiar characteristic.—G. J., June 29, 1878.

When a boy at home, as regularly as pancakes on Shrove Tuesday we expected fish for dinner on Good Friday, and veal, with lemon, followed by a custard, for dinner on Easter Sunday ; but I never heard any reason assigned. . . . Many people yet have veal at Easter ; but whether because it is then in season or not I cannot say. I do it merely from long habit, and because it reminds me of home and boyish days.—N. & Q.⁶, vol. vii., p. 238.

I was informed at the Easter of 1895 that in two villages in North Lincolnshire it was the custom to have for breakfast on Good Friday some of the liver of the calf, which is always killed the day before to provide veal for Easter Sunday. I never heard of this before and do not believe that the practice is at all a common one.—*Dublin Review*, 1898, p. 149.

Kirton-in-Lindsey. A laundress here refused to do any washing upon the day before Good Friday in this year [1897]. She said that ' if any one hangs out clothes to dry on Holy Thursday they will have bad luck all the rest of the year.' By 'year' was meant until the following Holy Thursday, not merely until the end of 1897. I have heard another woman here say it was unlucky to wash upon this day. Can some one give a reason for this belief? It does not apply to any other form of work; and so far as I can make out no other day in Holy Week has any similar superstition attached to it. Good Friday is, of course, observed as a holiday; that is, the shops are not open and the labouring men do not go to work; but it has always been the custom for them to set the potatoes in their own gardens upon this day.—N. & Q.⁸, vol. xi., p. 406.

The following story illustrative of the Lincolnshire superstition that persons born on Good Friday night cannot be frightened, was told me by a fellow-servant of its hero and its victim.

There was a lad living on the farm who had been born on Good Friday night, and who, therefore, could not be frightened, One of his mates determined to test his immunity, and, covering himself with a white sheet, waylaid him on a dark night in the churchyard. The lad coolly asked what he was 'fooling at' and knocked him down with a stick he was carrying. When he got home he was asked by some who were in the plot whether he had met anything. He replied that Jim had tried to frighten him, but that he had 'larned' him a lesson. As 'Jim' did not return to the house, he was sought for, and found dead. The 'lesson' had been effectual. This happened some forty or fifty years ago, I believe.—N. & Q.⁸, vol x., p. 92.

Good Friday, Shooting on.—See under FIFTH OF NOVEMBER.

On the 'Queen of Festivals' as also on Whitsunday we made a great point of appearing in Church in some new article of dress, being fully persuaded that

the little birds would mute their scorn upon us if
we were not careful thus to mark the occasion.—
G. J., June 29, 1878.

Clee. The parishioners present the Vicar, every Easter,
with a quantity of eggs collected in the parish; which
was anciently considered as a peace offering, but now
as a sort of commutation for the tithe of that article
throughout the year.—*Man. and Cus.*, p. 39.

Cheesecakes were held to be in season at Eastertide.
—G. J., June 29, 1878.

Holk Tuesday was the Tuesday fortnight after Easter-
day. . . . The men and women with great glee, on this
day, stopped the streets with long ropes, and entangling
the passengers, kept them in durance until they purchased their redemption by a small fine; and the stock
thus acquired was expended in a supper. In the above
feat the girls were the most active, and always produced
the greatest share of the booty.—OLIVER (3), p. 111.

In [Flete] street was celebrated annually the public
game of the Holk or Hock, which was derived from the
German *Hocken*, in reference to the custom of *binding*,
which was practised by the women upon the men on
Hock Tuesday, a fortnight after Easter. It was a merry
festival at which the female part of the community
reigned absolute. The young men and women amused
themselves on this day by stopping the streets round
the market-place, and seizing on the passengers, kept
them in durance until they purchased their emancipation
with a small fine. The stock of money thus acquired,
was expended in a feast at the close of the day. In
the execution of this feast the women were the most
active and always produced the greatest share of the
booty.—OLIVER, iv., pp. 197, 198.

All Fools' Day.—The buffoonery of April and Valentine days is so well known all over England, as to

N

render it unnecessary for me to say more than that it is not omitted in the county of Lincoln.—*Pop. Sup.*, p. 119.

On 'All-Fool's-Day,' April 1st, boys are sent to some ill-natured person for a 'penno'th of stirrup-oil,' which they sometimes get in the form of a beating with a stirrup leather.—E. PEACOCK, II., vol. ii., p. 525.

Grantham.—During the morning the fun was fast and furious, but tricksters calmed down in the afternoon as their victims had a right of reply in :

> 'Twelve o'clock is past and gone,
> And you're a fool for making me one.'

G. J., June 29, 1878.

St. Mark's-Eve, Divination on.—See SECTION VII.

Cf. also *Folk-Lore*, vol. xiv., p. 97.

Cattle kneeling on St. Mark's Eve.—See *Folk-Lore*, vol. xiv., p. 94.

Holy Thursday, or Ascension Day.—Thursday but one before Whit-Sunday; cannot fall before April 30, nor after June 2. This is the season when circuits of parishes are performed, in order to preserve and maintain their respective boundaries.—*Lincolnshire Cabinet*, 1829, p. 14.

Grimsby. The Church House, where the spits, crocks, and other utensils were deposited, that they might be ready for use at the Whitsuntide festival, when the young people met together for sports peculiar to the season, including boating, dancing, shooting at butts, etc., while the elders sat with their cans of ale before them to watch the games and settle disputes. A green arbour, called Robin Hood's bower, was put up in the churchyard opposite, where maidens gathered contributions. The Churchwardens brewed whitsun ales, and sold them *in the church*, distributing the profits to the poor inhabitants. This festival was kept in great state at Grimsby, and it is thus described by an eye-witness. An individual of each sex was previously chosen to be lord and lady of the feast, who dressed themselves in character; and the great tithe-barn was fitted up with seats for the company, decorated with garlands, ribbons, and other showy ornaments. Here they assembled towards the evening to dance and regale themselves, and each young man was expected to treat his girl with a ribbon or favour. The lord and lady were attended by the proper officers, and a jester dressed in a party coloured jacket, whose jokes and uncouth motions contributed to the entertainment of the company. The borough waits were also bound to attend with their instruments of music.—OLIVER, iv., pp. 151, 152.

Whitsun Ale.—An ale-feast at Whitsuntide.—E. PEACOCK, i., p. 277.

Whitsun Cake.—A kind of cake eaten at Whitsuntide, made of layers of paste, sugar and spices.—E. PEACOCK, II., vol. ii., p. 610.

Messingham. *May-tide.*—On May even, the lads and lasses of the village, this being the concluding evening of their year's servitude, assembled at Perestow Hills and amused themselves with all sorts of gambols, such as pat aback, dip-o'-the-kit and blind man's buff; they then, preceded by twangling Jack the fiddler, danced their way to the town, when every one dispersed to their respective parents or friends, for à few days' mirth and relaxation, before they again resumed the labours of another year's servitude. . . .—MACKINNON, pp. 11, 12.

May-Eve.—See also SECTION VII.

We watched for village children with their 'garlands,' pretty, fragrant, beflowered structures of the bower-type, which they carried about covered with a cloth and were proud to show at a half-penny a peep.—G. J., June 29, 1878.

Festivals.

Somerby, near Grantham. The first of May was observed in a very joyous manner by the young folks of this village. A number of children, sixteen in all, joined together in the collection of flowers, etc., and on Thursday morning they paraded the village, carrying on a pole, a large and handsome garland, which contained (in addition to the tasteful arrangement of flowers) a collection of fourteen dolls, the one representing the May Queen standing in the centre of the group. The proceedings were further enlivened by the children singing some favourite songs at the doors of the houses at which they asked to be remembered. In the afternoon, they sat down to a plentiful tea, which some kind friends had undertaken the trouble of arranging. The cost of the tea was defrayed out of the funds collected, and the balance was afterwards equally divided amongst the children. Another garland also deserves praise; this was accompanied by a missionary-box, and coppers were solicited on behalf of the missionary cause.—G. J., May 3, 1890.

Barnoldby-le-Beck. May Day was the village saturnalia; not May 1, but May Day by old style, May 13. Within the last twenty years we have heard in the village public shot after shot being fired behind the house for a kettle as a prize, while peals of laughter resounded through the still spring evening. Much fighting, drinking, and dancing went on at these village feasts thirty years ago; the 'lasses' ran races down the road for 'gown-pieces,' and donkey-racing was popular. The regular prizes for a donkey-race were: 1st, a bridle; 2nd, a pair of spurs; 3rd, a jockey's whip. A powerful farmer of the parish stopped these varied entertainments because in a wet hay-time the men would not work, and always stayed off their ordinary labour for two or three days' drinking; 'and a gude thing, too!' said a village wife, who told us of this suppression of the gaieties. [In a village five miles from Great Grimsby.]—*Antiquary*, vol. xiv., p. 11.

Festivals.

Old May-day.—The week after old May-day, is a feast held in the larger villages, the servants being at home with their friends.—*Lincolnshire Cabinet,* 1829, p. 14.

Lincolnshire Marsh. The first of May with all its old Maypole associations has no place left in Marshland now.* But when old Mayday comes then comes Carnival. It is the yearly hiring of farm servants. All those engaged at a yearly wage, and the maidservants in all but the best houses, take a week's holiday and rush from town to town in a constant whirl of amusement, which too often degenerates into debauchery. Out of many customs I may mention one connected with the hiring. No engagement holds till the hirer has handed over the fasten-penny, or earnest of the coming year's wage, and on this the recipient spits gravely ere he pockets it. Nowadays they spit for mere luck's sake, not knowing what they do. But it was, I believe, originally a charm against witches, who were supposed to 'eyespell' the first money paid away, but lost all power to do so after it had been placed in the mouth.—HEANLEY, p. 10.

South Kyme. There used to be a Queen of the May and great festivities on May Day.—FENLAND N. & Q., vol. iv., p. 325.

Lenton. *May-day Song.*—In May 1865, I gave in these pages a May-day song, as sung by children in Huntingdonshire (3rd S., vii., 373). Subsequently I was able to give a more extended version of the song (3rd S., ix., 388). Since then I have frequently heard the May-day children sing this song, with more or less of omission and variation. This last May-day I again heard it sung at Lenton, near Folkingham, South Lincolnshire, and I again took down the words. But they were very nearly

* Light, portable Maypoles are now carried round by bands of school-children at Kirton-in-Lindsey: but the modern May-Day observances have no connection with ancient tradition.—M.P.

the same as those given at my second reference. There was, however, this verse:

> Good morning, lords and ladies,
>   It is the first of May;
> We hope you'll view our garland,
>   It is so smart and gay.

The nightingale and cuckoo verse went thus:

> The cuckoo sings in April,
> The cuckoo sings in May,
> The cuckoo sings in June,
> In July she flies away.

This was succeeded by two verses which are quite new to me, and it is for the purpose of quoting them that I make this note:

> The cuckoo sucks the bird's eggs
>   To make her sing so clear;
> And then she sings 'Cuckoo'
>   Three months in the year.

In the third line the children imitated the cuckoo's double note:

> I love my little brother
>   And sister every day;
> But I seem to love them better
>   In the merry month of May.

The children told me that they were taught this song four years since by the daughter of the late master of the Board School.—N. & Q.[7], vol. i., p. 406.

The Huntingdonshire song was imparted to the children by a person who had learnt it from her mother 40 years before.

> Here come us poor Mayers all,
>   And thus we do begin—
> To lead our lives in righteousness
>   For fear we should die in sin.
>
> To die in sin is a fearful thing,
>   To die in sin for mourn;
> It would have been better for our poor souls
>   If we had never been born.

Festivals.

We have been rambling through the night,
    And part of the next day,
And, now we have returned back again,
    We have brought you a branch of May.

A branch of May it looks so gay,
    Before your door does stand.
It's only a sprout, but it's well budded out
    By the work of th' Almighty hand.

Awake, awake, my pretty fair maids,
    And take your May-bush in,
Or it will be gone ere to-morrow morn,
    And you'll say that we brought you none.

Awake, awake, my pretty fair maids,
    Out of your drowsy dream,
And step into your dairies all,
    And fetch us a cup of cream,

If it's only a cup of your sweet cream,
    And a mug of your brown beer;
If we should live to tarry in the town,
    We'll call another year.

Repent, repent you wicked men,
    Repent before you die,
There's no repentance to be had
    When in the grave you lie.

The life of man it is but a span,
    It flourishes like a flower;
To-day we are, to-morrow we're gone,
    We're gone all in one hour.

Now take a Bible in your hand,
    And read a chapter through;
And when the day of judgment comes,
    The Lord will think of you.

The nightingale she sings by night,
    The cuckoo she sings by day;
So fare ye well, we must be gone,
    And wish you a happy May.

Ropsley. The above song is also printed in the
Grantham Journal, May 9, 1903, after the following lines

relating to the parish of Ropsley, five miles east of Grantham.

Going a' Maying.—This old custom was observed by the children on the 1st of May. The garlands were made in the traditional oval shape, and were composed of cowslips, wood anemones, crab-blossom, wall-flowers, primroses, and daisies. Dolls were placed on the garland, the chief doll (though the children did not know it) being the representative of the goddess Flora, in the festival of the Roman Floralia. From the bases of some of the garlands, which were carried by means of a stick thrust through them, were hung ribbons and other gay-coloured material. The children took their garlands to the houses of the various residents, and sang their May-day song—a curious medley, in which religion figures after the manner of old times. The verses as at present rendered are given below : they have been handed down from mother to children, and have doubtless undergone considerable variation in the course of time :

AN OLD MAY SONG OF SIXTY YEARS AGO.

In reply to an enquiry in our columns for the words of an old May song, a correspondent sends the following, which, he says, ' we used to sing sixty years ago ' :

> Remember us poor Mayers all,
>   For here we do begin
> To lead our lives in righteousness,
>   For fear we should die in sin.
>
> For to die in sin what a sad thing is that—
>   To go where sinners mourn ;
> It would have been better for our poor souls
>   If we never had been born.
>
> Oh, take a Bible in your hand,
>   And go to Church and pray ;
> And when the Day of Judgment comes
>   The Lord will think of you.

Festivals.

For the life of a man it's no more than a span,
    It flourishes like a flower;
We are here to-day, to-morrow we are gone—
    We are all gone in one hour.

And when we are dead and in our graves,
    Our bodies to dust and clay,
The nightingale shall sit and sing
    To pass our time away.

Rise up, rise up, you pretty maids all,
    And out of your drowsy dream,
And step into your dairy-house
    And fetch us a cup of cream.

A cup of cream I do not mean,
    A bowl of your brown beer;
And if we should live to tarry in this town,
    We will call on you another year.

I have a purse, a pretty little purse,
    It draws with a silken string;
And all we want is a little silver
    To line it well within.

My song's begun and almost done,
    No longer can we stay;
So Heaven bless you all, both great and small,
    And send you a joyful May!

G. J., Apl. 22, 1905.

Grimsby. *May-Pole.*—Here [in the Bull-Ring] stood the shaft or Maypole, . . . and May-day was always kept as a public holiday. . . . It formed, I assure you, a very gay scene; the pole decorated with garlands of flowers, various coloured ribbons and streamers, green boughs and festoons of painted egg shells; while both lads and lasses appeared in fancy costumes; the queen of May outshining them all; being dressed very gaily and attended by several other girls who were called her maids of honour; she had also a young man called the captain, and under his command other inferior officers. And there was also Robin Hood, the friar, the fool, the dragon, and the hobby-horse, all robed in character. The body corporate enjoyed the privilege of cutting down a tree in Bradley Wood, for the May-pole, whence it was fetched betimes in the morning by the whole party, and brought into Grimsby with great rejoicing and much ceremony. After it was reared in the Bull-ring, and decorated from top to bottom, the whole youthful population fell to dancing round it as if they were mad, while the seniors enjoyed themselves with substantial eatables and drinkables that had been provided in the old tithe-barn for the occasion.—OLIVER, iv., pp. 189-190.

Hemswell May-pole.—On a recent visit to the neighbourhood of Gainsborough, I went to Hemswell, a village at the foot of what is termed 'The Cliff,' in the northern division of the county of Lincoln. In the centre of the village I was surprised to see a y-pole. The pole proper stands between two stout posts about fifteen feet high. Near the top of them a strong iron bolt is passed through the whole. The posts are fixed firmly in the ground, while the pole between is loose at the bottom, but kept in place by a second transverse bolt near the ground, which is drawn out when the pole is wanted to be lowered ; which is done by getting a ladder and fixing a rope high up on the pole, by which it is pulled down, swinging on the top transverse bolt as on a pivot. It is steadied by another rope at the bottom. When decorated it is raised to its place again by pulling the bottom rope, and it is fixed by reinserting the lower transverse bolt.—N. & Q.[8], vol. viii., pp. 184-185 ; WILKINSON, p. 167.

Horncastle. It is dubious whether Bowbridge has its name from the arch of the bridge, or from its being the entrance into the town from Lindum, through the gate formerly called a Bow. This way is the may-pole-hill. . . . The boys annually keep up the festival of the *Floralia* on May-day, making a procession to this hill with *May gads* (as they call them) in their hands : this is a white willow wand, the bark peeled off, tied round with cowslips, a *thyrsus* of the Bacchanals : at night they have a bonfire and other merriment ; which is really a sacrifice, or religious festival.—STUKELEY, i., p. 31 ; HISSEY, pp. 354-355 ; cf. *British Traveller*, p. 414, col. i.

A peculiar rustic ceremony, which used annually to be observed at this place, doubtless derived its origin from the Floral games of antiquity. On the morning of May-day, when the young of the neighbourhood assembled to partake in the amusements which ushered in the festivals of the month of flowers, a train of youths collected themselves at a place to this day called the *May Bank.* From thence, with wands enwreathed with cowslips, they walked in procession to the may-pole, situated at the west end of the town, and adorned on that morning with every variety in the gifts Flora. Here . . . they struck together their wands, and scattering around the cowslips, testified their thankfulness for that bounty, which . . . enabled them to return home rejoicing at the promises of the opening year. That innovation in the manners and customs of the county, which has swept away the ancient pastimes of rustic simplicity, obliterated about forty years ago [*i.e.* 1780] this peculiar vestige of the Roman Floralia. —WEIR, pp. 26-27.

The other evening I was walking in a lane and observed a number of children with linked hands form a revolving circle round an imaginary May-pole, all singing :

> All around the May-pole, trit, trit, trot ;
> See what a May-pole I have got ;
> One at the bottom and two at the top ;
> All around the May-pole, trip, trip, trop.

N. & Q.[4], vol. x., p. 106.

Kirton-in-Lindsey. *Stuffed Chine.*—At Kirton-in-Lindsey stuffed chine is eaten specially when the lads and lasses come home for a holiday at May-day, and also at the summer fair.—E. PEACOCK, i., p. 243.

Festivals.

May-Garlands.—See *Folk-Lore*, vol. ix., pp. 276, 365.

May-Poles.—See PART I., SECTION II.

Wigtoft. *May-light* [1505].—
  Itm. recevyd of yᵉ may lygthe of *Estthorppe*, o 3 3
        Accompts of Churchwardens, p. 199.

May-Day Peals.—NORTH, 236.

Lincoln. [May] 16 F. May-day market, is a great hiring of servants.—*Lincolnshire Cabinet*, 1828, p. 120.

May-hirings.—Between New and Old May day (sometimes earlier) high constables hold statues for hiring servants.—*Lincolnshire Cabinet*, 1828, p. 122.

May Day.—That is Old May Day, 13th May, from which the annual hiring of farm servants is reckoned.—COLE, p. 89.

[May-hirings are mentioned in E. PEACOCK, II., vol. ii., p. 345 ; *Lincolnshire Cabinet*, 1828, pp. 120, 122.

May-day.—The month before May-day, when scrubbing, whitewashing, and such like work, is done, before the old servants leave. In the Isle of Axholme, where the servants follow the Yorkshire custom of leaving their places at Martinmas, this work is frequently done in the Autumn, and is called 'the back-end cleaning up.'—E. PEACOCK, II., vol. i., p. 118.

Pag-rag Day.—The day when servants change their places at May-day or Martinmas.—THOMPSON, p. 717.

An old name for the day after May Day, that is, May 14th, when the farm-servants leave their places ; so-called from their 'pagging' or carrying away their bundles of clothes on their backs.—COLE, p. 106.

See E. PEACOCK, II., vol. ii., p. 393 ; WHEELER, Appendix IV., p. 11.

Festivals.

Pack-rag-day.—The 14th of May, the time when the servants in Lincolnshire pack up their clothes and change their places.—BROGDEN, p. 144.

Hatton. Bank Holidays pass almost unnoticed, but May 14th, or Pag-rag day, is a great event, when the single farm servants, male and female, leave their places, or at least take a week's holiday, and spend the time in visiting their friends and going round to the different markets. The married men decide whether they will remain with their masters at Candlemas; they have the privilege of attending what is called the labourer's market soon after that date, when they hire themselves again and leave their old places April 6th.—L. N. & Q., vol. v.: *Nat. Hist. Section*, p. 50.

Oak Day.—The 29th of May is Royal Oak Day all England over, and I only refer to it here because there is another custom also attached to that day in Marshland. It marks the close of the birds'-nesting season, the boys considering it most unlucky to take eggs later, and mostly abstaining from so doing.—HEANLEY, p. 11.

Grantham. On the 29th of May, 'Nettle Day,' we hardly dared to venture out if we lacked the protection of a sprig of oak, as we then incurred the risk of being stung by nettles as a punishment for not manifesting a loyal memory of King Charles the Second's well-known adventure. Some few cottages were made gay by oak branches being fixed to the hasps that fastened the shutters back against the wall.—G. J., June 29, 1878.

The 29th May, when school children wear oak leaves, and nettle those who have none; they have a rhyme. 'Royal Oak Day, Twenty-ninth of May, If you won't gie us a haliday, We'll all run away.'—COLE, p. 101.

Gainsborough. For some days previously the boys collect all the birds' eggs they can find or purchase, and early in the morning of the 29th, they may be seen returning from the woods in crowds, with an ample supply of oak. They next procure a large quantity of flowers, with which they construct a garland in the form of a crown, the apples of the oak being all gilded, surrounded by flowers and festoons of birds' eggs. The garland is then suspended across the street, and every little urchin being provided with a horn, some the natural horn of the cow, others of tin, similar to those formerly used by the guard of the mail coaches, they keep up throughout the day a most terrible blowing of horns, the doleful noise being ill in accordance with the festivity and rejoicing which the garlands are presumed to indicate. I have been unable to learn the origin or import of this singular custom.—N. & Q.[1], vol. v., p. 307.

Swineshead. 'Oak-apple Day' . . . is yet celebrated by the bells of Swineshead . . . and also by sprays of oak leaves being worn. . . . Some six or seven years ago many of the engines of trains running upon the Manchester, Sheffield and Lincolnshire Railway [afterwards the Great Central Railway] were decked with branches of oak on that day ; and it is no uncommon thing to see the plough boy adorn the heads of his horses with sprays of oak leaves in memory of King Charles's escape.—*Church Customs,* p. 34.

Clee. *Trinity Sunday.*—He who loves old forms and would keep the feast aright must dine upon stuffed chine and plate cheese-cakes at this season. . . . This village was famous in days of yore for its Mead.—WATSON, pp. 58, 59.

[Stuffed chine should also be eaten at the summer-fair, Kirton-in-Lindsey, and at Old May-day.]

Corpus-Christi.—See PART II., SECTION III., GAMES.

Winterton. A pleasure fair called 'Winterton Midsummer' is held at Winterton, in Lincolnshire, on 6th

July, and another 'Midsummer' is held on the same day
at Haxey, in the same county ; these feasts having nothing
to do with the dedication of the parish churches, they are
simply festivals held about the summer solstice (Old
Style).—N. & Q.[8], vol. ix., p. 48.

Sheep-clipping.—On the Wolds of Lincolnshire, the
farmers always provided 'frummaty' for breakfast at the
'clippins' (sheep shearings); but I never heard of its
being eaten at Christmas. . . . It was usual to give it, in
almost unlimited quantities, to the families of all the
labourers on the farm, to all the poor old women in the
village, also to the 'young ladies' at the Vicarage, in fact,
to almost every one within reach.—N. & Q.[5], vol. iv.,
p. 295. See WHEELER, Appendix IV., p. 7.

Frumity, Frumenty.—A pottage made of previously
boiled wheat, with milk, currants, raisins, spices, etc., once
commonly made by the farmers to be given away to their
neighbours on the sheep-shearing day.—BROGDEN, p. 74.

Lammas-day, which falls on the first of this month
[August], is one of the four *cross* Quarter-days of the
year, as they are denominated. Whitsuntide was formerly
the first of these quarters, Lammas the second, Martinmas
the third, and Candlemas the last ; and such partitions
of the year were once equally common as the present
divisions of Lady-day, Midsummer, Michaelmas, and
Christmas. Some rents are yet payable at these ancient
quarterly days in England, and they continue generally
in Scotland.—*Lincolnshire Cabinet,* 1828, p. 135.

Grimsby.—A bye-law of the Corporation provided that
upon St. Bartholomew's day [Aug. 24], when the mayor
went on his circuit, the Corporation and burgesses should
assemble with him in the chapel of St. Mary Magdalene,
and accompany him in his circuit about the town and
fields, and not be absent or depart from him without
licence under a penalty of fourpence. The day was

ushered in, . . . with ringing of bells and other solemnities. The mayor and his brethren, in their robes, met at the Hospitium where divine service was performed in the above chapel belonging to that house by the chaplain thereof, in which service the 103rd and 104th Psalms were always used. They then perambulated the parish, or *beat the bounds* as it was technically phrased ; that is to say, they proceeded round the utmost extremity of the parish, attended by a considerable number of the inhabitants, and claimed the whole as belonging to the lordship of Grimsby, to the exclusion of all other claimants. They scourged little boys at the holes where the soil had been thrown out to mark the boundary line, and then gave them a penny each to sharpen their memory of the several termini.—OLIVER, iv., pp. 142, 143.

Harvest Supper.—In portions of Lincolnshire . . . it is the custom for a farmer to give his men a supper at the end of the harvest, and this supper is locally termed 'horkey.'*—N. & Q.⁴, vol. vi., p. 387.

Frumerty, a preparation of creed-wheat [wheat simmered till tender] with milk, currants, raisins, and spices in it. Given to the servants at harvest suppers.—E. PEACOCK, i., p. 111.

Cf. *Folk-Lore*, xiii., 92.

Harvest-home.—In Lincolnshire hand bells are carried on the waggon ; and the rhyme runs :

> The boughs do shake and the bells do ring,
> So merrily comes our harvest in,
> Our harvest in, our harvest in,
> So merrily, etc.   NORTHALL, p. 262.

Harvest-lord.—The chief reaper.

Harvest-lady.—The second reaper, who supplies the 'lord's' place in his absence.—BROGDEN, p. 93.

---

* This word is, so far as I know, never used in North Lincolnshire, and Mrs. Gutch has never heard it near Grantham.

Festivals.

Lincolnshire Marsh. Harvest thanksgiving services have, I think, entirely supplanted the mell-supper in Marshland. When I was a boy every farmer held one, but now I do not know of a single survival. And old Dan Gunby, fowler and poacher, prince of scamps, but prince also of fiddlers, has been dead these twenty years, and with him have died the best traditions of the ' mell.'

But no further back than last September [1899], I saw a veritable ' kern baby '—a largish doll cunningly twisted out of barley straw, and perched up on a sheaf exactly facing the gate of the grand wheat-field in which it stood. I missed seeing the owner, a small freeholder, but mentioning the matter to an old dame (of whom a Marshman would say, ' them as knaws aal she knaws hezn't no need to go to no schule '). She made a reply which proves that, whatever else the Marshman has learnt of late to doubt, he still firmly believes in the Devil and his angels : ' Yis, she be thear to fey away t' thoon'er an' lightnin' an' sich-loike. Prayers be good enuff ez fur as they goas, but t' Awmoighty mun be strange an' throng wi' soa much corn to look efter, an' in these here bad toimes we moan't fergit owd Providence. Happen, it's best to keep in wi' both parties.'—HEANLEY, pp. 11, 12.

A lady who is a native of Lincolnshire tells me that in the first quarter of the present century ' the old sow ' used to appear in that county at harvest suppers. To the critical eye this curious animal was nothing more or less than two men dressed up in sacks to personate a traditional visitor to the feast. Its head was filled with cuttings from a furze bush and its habit was to prick every one whom it honoured with its attentions. ' I used to be very much afraid of it when I was a child ' says my informant. ' That was part of the harvest supper which I never could like.'—N. & Q.[8], vol. ix., p. 128.

'Last Sheaf' Rites.—. . . This 'nodding sheaf, the symbol of the god,' also assumes animal shapes. In Lincoln, for

instance, it is figured as an old sow or 'paiky.'—*Daily Chronicle*, 12 Sep., 1904.

Michaelmas-Day.—Mr. Wynne invited me on 'Minkleday,' Friday, September 29, 1876.—N. & Q.[5], vol. viii., p. 487.

Goose-feast.—Michaelmas. From the custom of eating geese on that day.—BROGDEN, p. 84.

Hopper-Cake Night.—Hopper, a large oblong basket, pendant from the shoulders of the husbandman, from which he scatters the seed when he sows the land.

It was anciently a custom with farmers to give a supper called 'hopper-cakes' (in which spiced cakes steeped in ale formed one of the chief viands, or delicacies), at the end of seed time, when the grain was finished being sown.—BROGDEN, p. 99.

Scotter. Cakes given to farm-servants and labourers when seed time is over. . . . Green, of Scotter, informs me that when he was a boy and young man, that is, between sixty and seventy years ago, hopper-cakes, or offer cakes, as they were sometimes called, were given away accompanied by spiced beer, at Scotter, by the farmers when the last seed was sown. It is to be feared that the custom and the name are alike obsolete.—E. PEACOCK, II., vol. i., p. 277.

Hot plum cakes, or seed cakes, given in former days with hot beer to the labourers on a farm on the completion of the wheat sowing. It was the custom to place them, and hand them round, in the empty Hopper or seed box, whence the name. So 'Hopper-cake Night,' the night when this was done.—COLE, p. 67.

Bottesford. *Nov. 5th.*—'A parishioner of mine was telling me last night—November 5th—that something like fifty or sixty years ago it was the traditional belief in this county and the neighbouring county of York that any farmer's son was at liberty to shoot on that day on his neighbour's farm, or in the preserves of his esquire, to his heart's content, and that, being November the 5th, there was no process of law by which he could be touched for so doing.' Such a belief was certainly current, only it extended further than my informant states. It was held that everyone—not farmers only—might shoot where they would on that day. I have heard my father say that when he was a lad and a young man—that is from 1805 to 1825—everyone who could procure a gun used to turn out, and that landowners and game preservers never thought of hindering them. The belief lasted much later. Somewhere about fifty years ago my father was riding to church on November 5th, when he met on the highway a notorious poacher, Jack Jackson, with his gun in his hand. My father, who had a liking for the man, pointed out to him the risk he was running. The man replied, 'No squire, I'm safe to-day. Don't you remember it's the 5th of November?' The same notion prevailed as to Good Friday ; but as it falls at a time when there is little game to be had, and what birds there are have become very wild, the people did not turn out in the same multitudinous fashion.—N. & Q.[7], vi., pp. 404, 405.

' *Shooting the Guy.*'—On the evening of November 5 the church bells were rung at Lenton and Ingoldsby, two adjacent villages in South Lincolnshire, and two or three sets of lads came to my door with their cry, ' Please to remember the fifth of November' as an excuse for begging. It was dark and raining heavily or the Lenton hand-bell ringers would have gone their rounds ; as it was, they kept in the belfry, where they were ringing and 'shooting' the bells. Children in the two villages explained that the bells were rung ' for shooting the guy.' No guys were brought round.—N. & Q.[8], vol. x., p. 426.

Festivals.

Fifth of November Customs.—See *Folk-Lore*, vol. xiv., p. 89.

All-Hallows.—An object called 'the idol of All-hallows' existed in the church of Belton in the Isle of Axholme in the early part of the reign of Queen Elizabeth. It was probably a representation of All Saints.—PEACOCK'S *Eng. Ch. Furniture*, 45 ; E. PEACOCK, i., p. 4.

Horsington. *All Saints' Eve.*—On the eve of All Saints Day, at 12 p.m., twelve lights rise from the mound in All Hallows Churchyard where the ancient church of Horsington stood (they are blue and rise slowly and do not jump about like jenny wisps), and then slowly proceed in threes towards the following neighbouring villages—3 to Horsington, 3 to Stixwould, 3 to Bucknall, and 3 to Wadingworth.—L. N. & Q., vol. iii., p. 209.

I. of Axholme. *Martlemas.*—Martinmas ; the feast of St. Martin, Nov. 11. Old Martinmas Day, the 23rd of November, is the time commonly observed by the people, and is the day on which new servants come to their places in the Isle of Axholme.—E. PEACOCK, II., vol. ii., p. 342.

Nov. 11.—. . . In former times May-day and Martlemas were periods like Lady-day and Michaelmas, Christmas and Midsummer, for the settling and auditing of biennial accounts. Martlemas-day, in old records, is generally called Saint Martin in Yeme, or St. Martin in the Winter. It is said that in whatever direction the wind may be on Martlemas eve, it is sure to continue in the same quarter for many weeks.—BROGDEN, p. 124.

Stirrup-Sunday.—That is Stir-up Sunday. The last Sunday after the feast of Holy Trinity, so called, it is said, on account of the first words of the collect in the Book of Common Prayer for that day : ' Stir up, we beseech Thee, O Lord,' which is a translation of a collect in the Salisbury use. On this day, or on the one following, the mince-meat for the Christmas pies, and the Christmas plum-pudding should be stirred by all members of the household.—E. PEACOCK, II., vol. ii., p. 525.

St. Thomas' Day. Gooding.—The custom of women going round to beg for corn or money on St. Thomas' Day against the Christmas Feast ; called also Mumping or Thomasing.—COLE, p. 56.

Cf. COLE, pp. 94, 152 ; BROGDEN, p. 131 ; E. PEACOCK, i., p. 175 ; II., vol. ii., p. 560 ; WATSON, p. 59.

St. Thomas's Day Custom.—It is customary in the Isle of Axholme, and I believe in the North generally for old women and others to 'go a-Thomasing on St. Thomas's Day, that is, asking for small doles of money or goods. In this neighbourhood they usually ask for and receive a candle apiece from the tradesmen who deal in such things. —N. & Q.[9], vol. v., p. 497.

South Lincolnshire. Old women called Mumpers, collect money, on St. Thomas'-day, when not on a Sunday.— *Lincolnshire Cabinet*, 1828, p. 152 ; 1829, p. 36.

Grimsby neighbourhood. Almost the only relaxation now comes from the lasses going home to see their mothers for a fortnight in May, and from going a-begging on St. Thomas's Day. Then all the old (and many of the young) women parade through the village, and call at all the substantial houses. The village shop perhaps gives them a candle apiece ; one farmer gives each family a stone of flour; another a piece of meat ; yet a third brews a quantity of hot elder-wine, and each woman has a glass and a piece of plum-cake. All well-to-do people give the widows a shilling each ; many are badgered into sending out five shillings, or even more, for the troop to divide as they choose. Then ensues, as may be expected, many a quarrel. The masterful obtain portions, the weak and poor get none. Yet this annual 'sportula' of Lincolnshire villages is much looked forward to and enjoyed.— *Antiquary*, xiv., 12.

Festivals.

In some counties corn used for furmety is given away, and this is called in Lincolnshire 'mumping wheat.'—*Old English Customs*, 1896, p. 29.

Christmas-tide. *Christmas-Eve.*—There was formerly a general custom, which I believe is still by no means extinct, of giving all animals better food on this day than that to which they were commonly accustomed. It is believed that at midnight on Christmas Eve all dumb animals kneel in reverence for the birth of our Lord. Many persons have assured me they have watched and seen the oxen in the 'crew yard' do this.—E. PEACOCK, i., p. 57.

. . . In a letter written by a Lincolnshire lady, 12 December, 1827, she refers to the management of a 'pig' to be bought ready killed, to provide 'pig-cheer' (as it is called) for Christmas (fry, sausages, pork pies, mince-pies etc. . . .—N. & Q.[10], iv., p. 449.

Our holy festival of Christmas retains in some parts of this island, particularly in Lincolnshire, the Saxon appellation of Yule. . . .—*Pop. Sup.*, p. 63.

Grimsby. Even at [Great] Grimsby, unlikely as it would seem among its multiform varieties of dissent, every Christmas produces a genuine survival of pre-Reformation belief. Children parade the streets and neighbouring villages bearing a wax-doll, laid in cotton-wool inside a box, and singing carols. They drop pence into the oyster-shell held out by the children.—*Antiquary*, vol. xiv., p. 10.

' *Vessel-cup* ' *or* ' *Crib.*'—See *Folk-Lore*, vol. ix., p. 365.

Hagworthingham. It. sometimes with the receipt of the Dancers gathering also of the young men calld the Wessell.—L. N. & Q., vol. i., p. 7.

In certain districts of the county of Lincoln, many of the old Christmas customs still prevail. At this season

the poor and indigent solicit the charitable aid of their
more wealthy neighbours towards furnishing a few necessary comforts to cheer their hearts at this holy but
inclement season. Some present them with coals, others
with candles, or corn or bread, or money. . . . In the
day-time our ears are saluted with the dissonant screaming
of Christmas Carols, which the miserable creatures sing
who travel from house to house with the *vessel-cup.* This
is a name given to a small chest, which encloses an image,
intended to represent the sacred person of our Saviour
Jesus Christ. Some of these vessels contain two figures
of different dimensions, to portray the Virgin and the
infant Saviour. In either case an apple is introduced
covered with gold leaf. It is reputed unlucky to dismiss
the singer without a present. The custom is rapidly
falling into disuse.

But Christmas Eve is the time of gaiety and good
cheer. The *yule-clog* blazes on the fire : the *yule-candle*
burns brightly on the hospitable board, which is amply
replenished with an abundance of *yule-cake* cut in slices,
toasted and soaked in spicy ale, and mince-pies, decorated
with stripes of paste disposed crossways over the upper
surface, to represent the rack of the stable in which Christ
was born ; and the evening usually concludes with some
innocent and inspiring game. A portion of the yule-cake
must necessarily be reserved for Christmas Day ; otherwise, says the superstition, the succeeding year will be
unlucky. A similar fatality hangs over the plum-cake
provided for this occasion, unless a portion of it be kept
till New Year's Day.—*Man. and Cus.*, pp. 28, 29.

Messingham. The seasons of festivity seldom occurred.
Christmas, Shrove Tuesday, Easter and the Feast were
the stated times. Then young and old came forth to
play. . . . Christmas, being a season of the year when
days are short and evenings long, and the wetness of the
low lands prevented the husbandman from following his

usual avocation, was kept for three weeks, and spent in social meetings at each other's houses. The yule log was now heaped round with peat-bags* and cassans,† and seen to sparkle on the cottage hearth, while the children listened with attention to their parents reciting the fun of former times, and the guests singing in their turns the carols of the season.—MACKINNON, pp. 9, 10.

Burning the *yule-clog* on Christmas Eve, giving *Christmas boxes* to children and to tradesmen's apprentices, etc., adorning the windows with *holly* and *evergreens*, and many other old customs, are still practised here.— *Axholme*, p. 280.

Yule-block, Yule-clog.—A great log or block of wood formerly placed with some ceremony upon the hall fire on Christmas Eve.

In former times (and the custom is perhaps still continued in some parts) the unconsumed part of the Yule-block was carefully preserved and re-placed on the fire to burn with the new one.—BROGDEN, p. 228.

Yule-clog, a log of wood put on the fire on Christmas Eve. Some portion of it should be preserved until New-Year's-Day, or evil luck will follow. My servant tells me, ' Father always saves a great block of wood to put on the fire at Christmas, and, isn't it curious, whatever sort of tree it comes from, he always calls it a *Yew*-log.'—E. PEACOCK, i., p. 279.

Mistletoe, Mistletoe-bough.—A bunch of evergreens, generally formed on a hoop. It is suspended from the ceiling at Christmas-tide, decked with oranges and trinkets, and is used for the same purpose as the real mistletoe in

---

* When peat was cut for fuel, the upper part, consisting of peat intermixed with roots of grass, was called *bags* ; the lower portion, which was peat only, went by the name of turves.

† Cow-dung dried for burning. Until the time of the great enclosures, cow-cassons supplied the poor with much of their fuel.

those parts of England where it can be readily procured. It is sometimes called a 'kissing-bough.'—E. PEACOCK, II., vol. ii., p. 354.

Christmas-Bough, and Christmas House-decorations.—See *Folk-Lore*, vol. ix., p. 364 ; vol. xiii., pp. 202, 203.

Christmas-Bough.—Cf. *The Christmas Bush*, N. & Q.[10], vol. iv., p. 502.

Christmas-Bough [For the use of 'an holy bush before the roode,' see *Church Gleanings*, p. 60].

I have recently been reminded that it is 'very bad luck' to burn the evergreens that have been used for Christmas decorations.—N. & Q.[8], vol. xii., p. 264.

Yule-caakes, Christmas cakes.—GOOD, p. 104.

Mince-pie.—It is said that *mince-pie* and *minch-pie* are not quite the same thing. *Minch-pies*, we are told, have meat in their composition ; *mince-pies* have not. It is commonly believed that if you eat twelve mince-pies before Christmas Day, you will enjoy twelve happy months in the coming year ; but if you eat fewer, you will have only as many as the number of mince-pies you have eaten.—E. PEACOCK, i., p. 171.

Goodying.—The practice of begging at Christmas.— BROGDEN, p. 84.

Clee. It is not necessary to place upon record that wait-singing by the younger folk . . . still heralds the approach of Christmas in this parish. Cleethorpes is especially blest in this respect.—WATSON, p. 59.

Christmas was celebrated . . . in a Church stuck about with little green bushes. . . . Our houses were decked with holly, box, fir, and laurel, and in some convenient spot the mystic mistletoe hung temptingly. In bed-chambers no 'Christmas' (evergreens) was permitted : it would have brought ill-luck, and to burn any of the refuse leaves was accounted a most dangerous provocation of—must I say?—the Fates. We had Waits who sang outside the house and School-children who entered in and refreshed themselves befittingly during the performance of their programme. I remember the time when Morris-dancers came from Belton. . . . On Christmas Eve a bowl was passed round, charged with a nauseous preparation of spiced ale, in which a round of toasted cake was floating. It was required of us to drink and to give utterance to a sentiment, not necessarily our opinion of the draught but something in the way of good wishes for the company. The elders played a rubber, and every now and then we were edified by hearing some of them threatening to turn their chairs in order to turn their luck, and if an unmarried person had bad 'hands' he would undoubtedly be consoled by the assurance that to be unlucky at cards is to be lucky in love . . . A large piece of wood called a yule-log was put on the fire on Christmas-eve and allowed to burn for a time, after which it was taken off and laid aside until New-Year's-eve when it might be utterly consumed. [I think it would be made to burn until after 12.0.] On that night many would remain up to sit the Old Year out and the New Year in. . . . The bells told us. when the fateful moment came.—G. J., June 29, 1878.

Evergreens are placed in churches, etc., on Christmas-day.—*Lincolnshire Cabinet,* 1828, p. 153; BROGDEN, p. 41 ; E. PEACOCK, II., vol. i., p. 113 ; also referred to p. 182, and vol. ii., pp. 417, 523, 587.

Lincolnshire Marsh.—The most vigorous survival of custom . . . is at Yuletide. . . . Preparations begin betimes, and everyone in the house down to the infant in arms must stir the pudding and the mincemeat, and though the mistletoe itself grows not in marshland, a bunch of evergreens that is called 'The mistletoe,' and has the same functions and privileges attached to it, is hung up in every farm kitchen. When Christmas Eve has come the Yule cake is duly cut and the Yule log lit, and I know of some even middle-class houses where the new log must always rest upon and be lighted by the old one, a small portion of which has been carefully stored away to preserve a continuity of light and heat. And, whilst the widows of the place have received their Yuletide gifts on St. Thomas's Day, going a Thomassing from farm to farm, go where you may between Christmas Day and Twelfth Night, into farm house or cottage, you will be pressed to taste a bit o' cake and cheese ; and whilst it is dire offence to refuse, your self-martyrdom is encouraged by the remembrance that for every bit you taste one more happy month is added to your life!—HEANLEY, p. 6.

Mumby. *Christmas Eve.*—In former times a Yule block was to be found on every fire : whilst on the table the Yule candle (a big candle, shopkeepers used to give to their customers at this time) burned with, what was in the days of rushlights and farthing dips, a wondrous light. Cakes and hot spiced beer were served, the plum cake being cut into long strips and dipped into the beer. This is still done in some public houses. The churches were decorated with box and other evergreens stuck into holes in the pew tops. Several old people here remember this church being so decorated, and call it 'sticking the church.' Our bells still ring on Christmas Eve ; years ago they commenced at 5 a.m. on Christmas Day, now it is 8 a.m. Frumerty lingers as a recollection, but seems to have been more connected with sheep clipping time. The carol singer is unknown ; the only trace I can find so far is the following, taken down from the lips of a very old man in the neighbourhood :

> All ye that are to mirth inclined,
> Consider well, and bear in mind
> What our good Lord for us has done,
> In sending His beloved Son.

Festivals.

The night before the happy tide,
Our spotless Virgin and her guide
Were long time seeking up and down
To find some lodging in the town.

But mark how all things came to pass.
No resting-place for them there was ;
Nor could they rest themselves at all,
But in a hungry oxen stall.

That night the Virgin Mary mild
Was safe delivered of a Child,
According to Heaven's decree
Man's sweet salvation for to be.

There were three kings all in the East,
Were tempted by a cheery star,
Came bearing down and made no stay
Until they came where Jesus lay.

This clearly needs revision, but that is the business of the folk-lore collector, and therefore I give exactly as reported to me.

The week before Christmas the morris dancers used to come round. There were several actors : 1st Tom Fool, dressed in imitation rags and tatters, with big yellow letters T. and F. on his back ; 2nd, the lady (or witch) a man dressed in hat and veil and gaudy sash round the waist ; 3rd, a fiddler, generally dressed in a red coat ; 4th, the farmer's son, a bit of a dandy ; and two others, dressed 'a bit comical.' When the party came to a house they proposed visiting, Tom Fool went in and said :

' Here comes I that's niver been yet,
With my great head and little wit.
A noä what my wife en me likes best,
En we'll hev it, too : a leg ev a lark, en the limb of a loose,
En cut a great thumpin' toast offen a farden loaf.'

If Tom Fool saw he was welcome, they all came in and sat down, Tom Fool taking care to be near the lady, whom he courted with much palaver and 'dittiment'; their

sweet converse was then stopped by the farmer's son, who
began to court the fair dame, telling her 'she mun nivver
tek up wi' a critter like that,' as he could never keep her,
etc. So poor Tom Fool got the sack, and went and
stood in a corner and openly bewailed his hard fate.
After a bit the farmer's son moved off, and Tom Fool
came back and declared if she would only have him she
'sud ha' bacon fliks, and flour i' th' bin, en ivverything, if
she wain't tek notice a' that chap wi' his ruffles en dangle-
ments.' At last they agreed to marry, which ceremony
was performed in a corner, one of the actors being parson.
The wedding was then celebrated in dance and song ;
after that bread, cheese, beer, etc., was given to the
players, who then retired and went elsewhere to 'say their
piece.' The songs I have not been able to get hold of,
but [they] appear to have been variable and dependent on
the original actor's taste.

'A young man went to see his sweetheart, en wen
'e got there 'e says : "A've cum t' cum t' the', t' see
the', to tell the' t' ask the' t' hem'ma ? What saays
th', sweetheart ? Wilt th' hem'ma ?" "Noa, not I."
"Nor I, neyther ; bud oor foäks wud hem'ma t' cum
t' the' t' see the', t' tell the', to ask the' t' hem'ma ?"'
After this, another friend favoured as follows : 'Es aw
sat i' mi' titterty tatterty, lukking oot i' mi hazy-gazy.
Aw sah a rueri run away wi' randy pipes. If aw'd
had mi striddlestripes on, aw'd ha maade rueri put randy
pipes doon ;'* or, according to another variant :

> 'Es aw looked out i' my asey-casey,
>   On a moonlight night,
> Aw sah th' dead carrying the live.
>   Wasn't that a wunderful sight ? '

Of the rest I can select but one. 'In olden days
they used to fetch their servants home on horseback.

---

* That is ; when I got up and looked out of the window, I saw a fox
running away with a goose, and if I had my trousers on, I'd have made
him put goose down.

Festivals.

One master, on the way thus begins a chat with his new maid :—"What de ye caal me, Mary?" "Meyster, sor." "Ye shuddn't caal me meyster, ye shud caal me Domine Sceptre." Soä, as they was goin' home the' came to th' pit, soä he saays, "What de ye caal that, Mary?" "Water, sor." "Ye shuddn't caal it watter, ye shud caal it absolution." Soä when the' got home, he says, "What de ye caal that, Mary?" "Hoose, sor." "Ye shuddn't caal it hoose, ye shud caal it high top o' th' mountain." Soä wen th' got inte th' hoose he saays, "What de ye caal that, Mary?" "Cat, sor." "Ye shuddn't caal it cat, ye shud caal it white-faaced Timothy." Soä he saays, "What de ye caal that, Mary?" "Fire, sor." "Ye shuddn't caal it fire, ye shud caal it Hococogloriam." Es they wes goin' up-stairs, he saays, "What de ye caal these, Mary?" "Steps, sor." "Ye shuddn't caal them steps, ye shud caal them wudden upps." Soä wen they got upstairs, he says, "What de ye caal this, Mary?" "Bed, sor." "Ye shuddn't caal it bed, ye shud caal it Ashedecree." Soä he took off his slippers, en says, "What de ye caal these, Mary?" "Slippers, sor." "Ye shuddn't caal them slippers, ye shud caal them groond tredders. What are these, Mary?" "Trousers, sor." "Ye shuddn't caal them trousers, ye shud caal them small clothes." Soä next mornin' she goäs agen th' steps en saays [or beäls oot or squeäls] "A', Domine Sceptre, get oot i' yer ashedecree, en put on yer smaal clothes en groond tredders, en cum down th' wudden upps te me ; for white-faaced Timothy hes got sum hococogloriam on his back, en withoot th' help of absolution, th' high top o' th' mountain will soon be one mass of hococo-gloriam."

'Them's real owd isrums,' quoth one of my Lincoln-shire friends, when I read them over to him to see if they were correct. The rest of the 'isrums' must find place another day.—L. N. & Q., vol. ii., p. 23.

Festivals.

Grimsby. [Temp. Hen. VI.] Sir Richard Tunstall . . . kept Christmas eve with great hospitality, surrounded by his friends and retainers. The Yule log blazed on the hearth; the boar's head was introduced with the sound of trumpets; and above all, at the proper season, he patronised the sport of the Plough Ship; which was formally authorized by an especial edict of the Corporation; which provided that all manner of actions shall be made in this borough upon these days following, that is to say, the Saturday from sunrise to the Sunday at two o'clock in the afternoon; to endure from Yule, beginning at noon, to the morning after *Plough Ship*, which shall be led about the town, etc. This Plough Ship . . . was a combination of the ancient pageant and the morris dance; and Maid Marian and the Fool were considered indispensable appendages to the *dramatis personæ.* . . . The young fellows dressed themselves in fantastic habits, dragging after them a plough, and solicited the benevolence of the inhabitants that they might enjoy a feast at the commencement of the new year. . . . The procession started from the Hall-garth. . . . The performers repeated a kind of dialogue, and were accompanied by the Corporation waits. The custom was continued down to a very recent period; and in the year 1724 an earthquake, accompanied by a storm of wind and rain, occurred between the villages of Laceby and Aylesby, which so frightened the Grimsby morris dancers that they took to their heels, and scampered away home with the utmost precipitation, under an apprehension that evil spirits were about to punish them for mockery in their sports. It [the Plough Ship] was accompanied by the sword dance.—OLIVER, iv., pp. 177, 178, 179.

Sleaford. Morris dances . . . are still practised in this neighbourhood, though not with the zest of former times. This pastime is a combination of the ancient pageants and the morisco dance ; and Maid Marian and the Fool are considered as indispensable appendages to the party. It is an antique piece of mummery, performed at Christmas, as a garbled vestige of the sports which distinguished the Scandinavian festival of Yule. The performers repeat a kind of dialogue in verse and prose which is intended to create mirth, and ends in a comic sword dance, and a plentiful libation of ale.—OLIVER (3), p. 117.

In the Christmas sports still used in this county, St. George thus introduces himself :

> ' Here comes I, St. George,
> That worthy champion bold,
> And with my crown and spear
> I won three crowns of gold.
>
> I fought the dragon bold,
> And brought him to the slaughter,
> By that I gained fair Sabra
> The King of Egypt's daughter.'
>
> OLIVER (3), pp. 83, 84.

Wainfleet. *Sword Dancers.*—The ' guisers,' or sword dancers, still come round. We had one family in Wainfleet Flats who were especially skilled in the intricacies of the dance, although they flatly refused to let me take down the verses they used, as ' some harm would happen them if they committed them to writing.' But whilst the words and the subject of the song have plainly varied with the times, the dance is as clearly a relic of the Norsemen and their war dances. For instance, the last time they visited me at Wain-fleet, just ten years ago, one of the company was dressed in skin with a wisp of straw in his mouth so cut as to represent a pig's bristles, thus recalling the hog sacrificed of old to Odin ; but for many years the 'Plough bullocks' that are due on Plough Monday have ceased to carry with them the horse's skull that used to represent the white steed Gleipnir of the ancient god. Indeed, I do not think I have seen that since 1857, when the general rejoicings at the close of the Crimean war gave a temporary fillip to the winter's sports.

It is, I suppose, generally allowed that the Plough bullocks represent the Wild Huntsman and his rout. Be that as it may, at this season of the year great numbers of wild geese daily cross Marshland, flying inland at early dawn to feed, and returning at night. No one who has heard their weird cry in the dusk can feel surprised that the older labourers still speak with bated breath of the 'Gabblerout' of the Wild Huntsman, and the wandering souls of children who have died without baptism whom he chases, and whom you may see for yourselves as 'willy wisps' flitting across the low grounds most nights of the year.—HEANLEY, pp. 6, 7.

Morris-Dancing.—The ceremony of *dancing the morris*, has but recently been discontinued.—PECK, *Axholme*, p. 278.

Morris-dancers, persons who perform rude plays; now much the same as 'plough-boys,' though formerly there was a clear distinction. [See under PLOUGH MONDAY.] —E. PEACOCK, i., p. 173.

A person who is born on Christmas Day will be able to see spirits.—N. & Q.[1], vol. viii., p. 382.

The canniness of the personal touch at the end is delightfully characteristic of the old Lincolnshire Marshman.—L. N. & Q., vol. vi., p. 115.

FAIRS AND FEASTS.

Comassing.—Begging at fair times.—*Scotter* ; E. PEACOCK, II., vol, i., p. 131.

Stattis.—The Statutes, or Statute Fair, such as at May Day, at which farm-servants are hired for the year.— COLE, p. 141.

Boston. Here is held one of those annual Fairs, which preserve the antient Title of a *Mart*, whereof I remember only four in *England* of any considerable note, *viz. Lynn, Gainsborough, Beverly,* and *Boston.* Its trade of late years has not increased —DEFOE, vol. ii., p. 342.

Bourn. Here are also three fairs, but they are only nominal ones ;—one is on the 7. March, another on the 6. of May, and the other on the 29. of October. This last is a great Wake.—MARRAT, vol. iii., 83.

Dyke is a hamlet to Bourn. It consists of about 30 houses, and has an annual Feast or Wake in July. —MARRAT, vol. iii., p. 84 [misprinted 81].

Brothertoft. So long as the Common continued open, it was the annual custom for the Fen reeves to assemble on the 8th of July O.S. and drive to Brothertoft such sheep as were found in their wool, and to levy a fee of four pence per head on such as belonged to persons having no Common-right, at which time commenced, and continued for a week, the feast, or festival called *Toft Drift.*

On this occasion Brothertoft was the resort of thousands of Persons from Boston and the surrounding Villages, for whose accommodation about 30 large Booths were erected where Ale, and Provisions were vended, while many hundreds were entertained, during the week, by the open door hospitality of the Inhabitants.

Anciently the Booths were erected on the West of Brothertoft, but, from about the year 1 7 0 [*sic*] they were fixed on the East.—MARRAT, vol. ii., Additions and Corrections.

Clee. It was, within my remembrance, celebrated with great merriment for three or four days; and the evenings were spent in dancing and other rational amusements. . . . Thus the Feast of Dedication at Clee was held on Trinity Sunday, and the week following, in the Churchyard, for many centuries after the prohibitory statute of 13 Edw. I. had made the custom penal; and a singular practice still prevails, which has been continued by prescription from a remote period of antiquity; probably from the time when the Church was dedicated, as it is a usage which was commonly practised on such occasions. On the feast Sunday the Church is gaily strewed with fresh mown grass, the fragrance of which is extremely grateful; and on that day the congregation is generally very numerous.—*Man. and Cus.*, p. 37.

In the *Clee-cum-Cleethorpes Parish Magazine* for July [1897] I find the notice ' Parish Church Trinity Sunday was marked by the ancient ceremony of strewing the Church with grass.' The rector Canon Hutchison explains: 'The Clerk says that about four acres of land were left as glebe, on condition that the Church was strewed with rushes (the field produced little else) on Trinity Sunday. This land was exchanged for other acres by the Enclosure Act, but the custom is still kept up, owing I suspect from the clerkship having descended from father to son for many years. The present clerk's grandfather was born about 1750. My informant seemed to think that the strewing the rushes was in virtue of the acknowledgment of a rent ; but, of course, it is quite possible that the benevolent individual who left the land may have wished the old mud floor of the Church to be made decent for 'Feast' Sunday.—N. & Q.[8], vol. xii., p. 274 ; E. PEACOCK, i., p. 242 ; SLEAFORD, 1825, p. 196.

See PART II., SECTION III., GAMES, under *Play-garth.*

Cf. WHITE, p. 278 ; *Curiosities of the Church,* p. 61.

Rush-strewing in Churches.—Cf. *The Antiquary,* vol. xxxv., p. 177.

Crowland. '*Saint Rattle Doll Fair.*'—The annual Shrove Tuesday Fair at Crowland, Lincolnshire, has gone by the singular name of 'Saint Rattle Doll.' I do not know in what way the word ' doll ' was imported into the title ; but the 'rattle' was the rattling of dice for nuts and oranges, and this species of gambling was very popular, and formed the chief attraction of the fair. 'Saint Rattle Doll,' however, now exists more in name than in fact ; and on the past Shrove Tuesday, 1877, the fair was only represented by one stall.—N. & Q.[5], vol. vii., p. 166.

Grantham. *Fairs.*—

1. Fair, and the most ancient, is that of Oct. 15 (by change of style, the 26th), in memory of St. Wulfran.

2. On the Monday before Palm Sunday in Lent, commonly called Caring Fair.

3. On Ascension day, commonly called Holy Thursday Fair.

4. On St. Peter's day, June 29 (now July 10), granted by King Charles at the renewing the charter.—MARRAT, vol. iv., p. 64.

The [principal] Fair . . . began on the Monday after the Fifth Sunday [in Lent] (popularly known as Fair Sunday). . . . Most of the caravans were fresh from

Stamford where the children had had their pleasure the week before. We used to say 'Fine at Stamford (fair) wet at Grantham,' and *vice versa.*—G. J., June, 29, 1878.

Forty Feast Sunday, always falls on the Sunday after the 10th of July, and is so called, it is said, because forty feasts occur on that day.—G. J., July 13, 1889.

Haxey. A feast, or pleasure fair, is held on July 6th. On Twelfth Day (January 6th), the rustics amuse themselves with an ancient game, called 'throwing the hood.'—WHITE, p. 405.

Heckington. We were not a little surprised at finding in the customs of this place, a departure from the general and almost universal usage of holding the feast-day on the day of the dedication of the church. Here we have four entire calendar months intervening between the annual feast—the Sunday after Magdalen (twenty-second of July)—and St. Andrew (thirtieth of November).—SLEAFORD, 1825, p. 252.

Horncastle. *Horse Fair.*—Now held on the second Monday in August and four days following.—L. N. & Q., vol. i., p. 86.

The second [fair], which terminates on the twenty-first of August, has long been celebrated as the largest fair for horses in the kingdom, perhaps it may be said in the world; it continues about ten days, being three days more than the time expressed in the charter.—WEIR, p. 40.

For these strangers were many of them, accomplished horsemen . . . and it has been pointed out as a significant fact that the greatest horse-fairs in England are still held at Horncastle and Howden—one in Lincolnshire, the other in Yorkshire, but both alike in the very heart of Danish England.—STREATFEILD, p. 52.

Kirton-in-Lindsey. *T' Andra' Fair*, the fair held at Kirton-in-Lindsey on the feast of St. Andrew, old style.

Local Customs.

The Parish Church is dedicated to Saint Andrew.—
E. PEACOCK, i., p. 249.

Little Fair Day.—The pleasure fair, or second day of
the fair at Kirton-in-Lindsey and Brigg.—E. PEACOCK,
II., vol. ii., p. 326.

Lincoln. The September fair was chartered for three
days, Wednesday, Thursday, and Friday, but is now only
held on the latter day. It is sometimes called All Fools'
Fair, from a tradition that William III., when he granted
it to the Corporation after they had given him a sumptuous
entertainment, styled them 'all fools' for not asking him
for something better. The November fair is sometimes
called Hugh fair, from its being formerly held in a close
called St. Hugh's croft.*—WHITE, p. 500.

Messingham. A few days before the feast, the outside
of the houses are washed over with stone-colour wash ;
this gives an uniform appearance, and contentment ; com-
fort and cleanliness reign throughout the village.—
MACKINNON, pp. 25, 26.

Navenby. Fair, for wooden and brazier's ware [12th
April].—*Lincolnshire Cabinet,* 1827, p. 78.

Nettleham. About three miles north-east from the city
of Lincoln is a populous village called Nettleham, which,
like most others, has its annual wake, or feast. This is
held at Easter, and called the *Flaun,* from the custom, as
I should conceive, of eating flauns.†—*Man. and Cus.,*
p. 225.

There is no doubt . . . that the euphonious name of
that celebrated rural festivity [Nettleham Flawn], is
derived from the circumstance of it being held at Easter,
just when the severities of Lent might be supposed to

---

* St. Hugh's day is Nov. 17th, New Style, and the fair is on the 28th,
St. Hugh's eve, Old Style.

† Cheesecakes are a favourite dish at many village feasts.

have rendered a return to more savory diet a very agreeable thing. The *Flavonis penni*, or Flaun's-penny, given formerly at Easter, was probably expended in some such cates as the above-mentioned *Porken Flaunpeynes.*— *Topographical Society*, p. 64, note.

Scopwick. The village feast, which is celebrated in the week after Old Holy Rood, still retains some vestiges of ancient hospitality; and the most ample preparations are made in the preceding week for the important solemnity. Every cottage undergoes a thorough scarification. Mops, brooms, and whitewash, are in high request and such scrubbing and scouring are not witnessed at any other season of the year ; no, not at the formidable May-day. Each plaister floor is washed white, and decorated with a running pattern in black, produced from a composition of soot and water, to imitate a carpet or floorcloth. The visitors are expected with an eager anxiety ; nothing else is talked of amongst the housewives of the village ; every other consideration is absorbed in anticipation of the approaching week ; and on the Saturday evening, a general delivery of game, provided by the liberality of Mr. Chaplin, the proprietor of the lordship, takes place, and every cottage is furnished with a hare for the solace of its inmates. . . .—*Man. and Cus.*, p. 36.

Stamford. According to a charter of King Edgar in 972 Stamford then enjoyed a market ; and Henry II. granted to the town right to take market tolls, which were paid at sound of bell. Fifty years ago it was customary for farmers and factors to begin bargaining at the tinkling of a hand-bell.—BURTON, p. 79.

Corpus Christi Fair, Monday after that day.—*Lincolnshire Cabinet*, 1828, p. 124.

Stow Green. Stow Green fair, which is upon the Roman highway accompanying the Carsdike.—*Stukeley Corr.*, ii., p. 343.

Local Customs.

Stow, a hamlet in the parish of Threckingham consisting of but three or four houses, is situate about half a mile south-west of it, and adjoins the old road or Hermen Street. . . . A fair is annually held here, on a remarkable piece of ground called Stow Green Hill, for cattle and all kinds of tradesmen's goods, on the fourth of July, besides another on the fifteenth and sixteenth of June for horses only. These fairs, it is conjectured, were both as one, and formerly held the whole time of the intermediate days, for a toll is still paid for all carriages that pass over the hill between the fifteenth day of June and the fourth of July in each year.

This fair is said to have originated in commemoration of the beforementioned battle with the Danes on or near the above piece of land ; however, be that as it may, it is certain that a fair has been held here now near eight hundred years, as one of the extracts from the Conqueror's Survey, introduced in our account of Threckingham, says, 'There is a fair yielding forty shillings.'—SLEAFORD, 1825, p. 356.

A fair, said to have arisen from the above circumstance [the killing of three Danish kings at Threckingham], is annually held at *Three-king-ham* on a remarkable piece of ground, called *Stow Green Hill*, reported to be the spot whereon the battle was principally contested, and Domesday-book in some degree corroborates the statement ; for in the Conqueror's time, A.D. 1080, when that survey was taken, we find that there was then a fair held here. . . . This fair, however, is not held now in the month of September [when the battle was fought], but commences on the 15th of June, and continues till the fourth of July, and was very probably changed in the fifty-second year of the reign of King Henry III., who according to Tanner's *Notitia Monastica*, granted a charter for a fair at this place to the monastery of Sempringham.—HONE, *Every-Day Book*, vol. ii., p. 624.

Fairs and Feasts.

At Stow Green Hill, near Treckingham by the foundation of an old chapel, a great fair is annually held for cattle and all kinds of tradesmen's goods on July 4, besides another on June 15 and 16 for horses only. These fairs, it is thought, were both as one, and formerly held the whole time of the intermediate days ; and a toll is still paid for all carriages which happen to pass over the hill between the above days, June 15, and July 4, in each year. A fair was granted to the monastery of Sempringham, to be held at this place, by charter 52 Henry III.*—*Topography*, p. 180.

Kirton-in-Lindsey. *Church Ale.*—Something in the nature of a church ale . . . at Kirton-in-Lindsey, existed until within my own memory. The church-house had long been swept away, and no money for the fabric was raised by the ale, but the salary of the sexton was in part paid by a feast given at his house, to which all persons could go who were willing to pay for what they consumed. How the licensing laws were evaded or suspended I do not know.—E. PEACOCK, *Church Ales*, p. 14.

Barley and Malt.—Extracts from the Churchwarden's Accompts of Wigtoft.—MARRAT, vol. i., pp. 198, 199.

Bardney. *Bread Doles.*—Money or bread distributed to the poor, formerly at funerals, and now through the bequests of deceased persons. . . . There are doles for the parish of Bardney, Lincolnshire.—BROGDEN, p. 55 ; MARRAT, vol. vi., pp. 127, 128.

Bourne. On Friday evening week Mr. W. E. Lawrence let by auction the piece of land termed the ' White Bread Meadow,' containing about five roods, and situate in the Meadow Drove in Bourn North Fen. On this occasion Samuel Nixon was the highest bidder at £5 15s. A

---

* Tanner's *Notitia.*

novel custom exists in connection with the management and administration of this charity. On the evening of the letting, which takes place annually, the auctioneer proceeds to the Queen's Bridge, in the Eastgate, where the company meet him, and the auction commences: a boy, who is called a 'runner,' is sent about fifty yards down the Eastgate, and returns to the starting point; if during his run any further bid is made, another boy is started, and so on ; but if the 'runner' returns before any advance is made upon the previous bid, the auction is declared to be at an end. The parishioners of the Eastgate appoint two stewards, who on the day of the letting purchase between £4 and £5 worth of penny and two-penny loaves, and distribute them in quantities of from a pennyworth to fivepennyworth at each house in what is considered the Eastgate ward. Until this year it has been the custom to leave the bread at these houses only which were said to be old houses ; this year a portion was left at every house in the Eastgate district. At the close of the auction the company proceed to one of the Eastgate inns to 'take a leetle refreshment.' Bread and cheese and onions, ale in abundance and of excellent quality, is brought in, and ample justice is done thereto by the company ; who by this time have become rather numerous, and each one on good terms with himself, if not with everyone else. Then follows the business of the evening: the stewards receive the rent, pay the expenses incurred, and then favour the meeting with the following 'state of affairs,' namely, balance in hand from the last year, 1s. 5d, this year's rent £5 15s; total, £5 16s. 5d. On the other side there was—paid for bread, £4 5s. ; the two stewards, 2s. 6d. each ; auctioneer, 5s. ; crier, 1s. ; bottle of gin, 2s. 6d. (to stimulate the bidding at the auction); and 17s. 6d. for cheese, onions, and ale, to balance the account. This left 5d. in hand, which it was suggested should be spent in tobacco ; to this, however, the stewards objected, being in favour of

retaining this balance in hand until the next letting.*—
N. & Q.[8], vol. i., p. 482 ; *ib.*[10], vol. iii., p. 365.

www.ingramcontent.com/pod-product-compliance
Lightning Source LLC
Chambersburg PA
CBHW020358270326
41926CB00007B/501